CELEBRATING MIDDLE-EARTH

An Examination of the Writings of J. R. R. Tolkien
as a Defense of the Literary, Philosophical, Political,
and Religious Foundations of Western Society

Other Books from Inkling

Theism and Humanism by Arthur J. Balfour

In 1962, *Christian Century* magazine asked C. S. Lewis to name the books that had most influenced his thought. Among them was this book. "My desire," Balfour wrote, "has been to show that all we think best in human culture, whether associated with culture, goodness or knowledge, requires God for its support, that Humanism without Theism loses more than half its value." Long out of print, the book that Lewis once praised as "too little read," is now available to all who are intrigued by the relationship between science and religion.

ISBN: 1-58742-005-8 (pb) 1-58742-016-3 (hb)

Eugenics and Other Evils by G. K. Chesterton

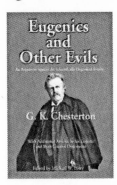

In the early decades of the twentieth century, eugenics, the scientific control of human breeding, was a popular cause within progressive segments of Western society. Few dared to criticize it and fewer still had the courage to launch a sustained attack on what the *New York Times* praised as a wonderful "new science." Perhaps the boldest of its critics was G. K. Chesterton, who warned that, "the creed that really is proclaimed not in sermons but in statutes and spread not by pilgrims but by policeman — that creed is the great but disputed system of thought which began with Evolution and has ended in Eugenics."

ISBN: 1-58742-002-3 (pb) 1-58742-006-6 (hb)

Chesterton Day by Day by G. K. Chesterton

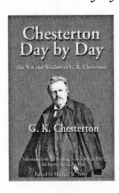

G. K. Chesterton will never become irrelevant. His words have the remarkable ability to remain as fresh and stimulating today as they did on the day he wrote them. Here, selected by Chesterton himself, are portions of his writings from 1901 to 1911, one for each day of the year. New to this edition are notes giving the background to his remarks and a detailed index. Read again remarks such as, "Modesty has moved from the organ of ambition. Modesty has settled upon the organ of conviction—where it was never meant to be. A man was meant to be doubtful about himself, but undoubting about the truth."

ISBN: 1-58742-014-8 (pb) 1-58742-015-5 (hb)

These books are available online or through any bookstore (wholesale from Ingram or Baker & Taylor). More information at www.InklingBooks.com

CELEBRATING
MIDDLE-EARTH

The Lord of the Rings as a Defense of Western Civilization

Edited by

John G. West, Jr.

Inkling Books   Seattle   2002

Celebrating Middle-earth: The Lord of the Rings *as a Defense of Western Civilization* is based on speeches given at the "Celebrating Middle Earth" conference at Seattle Pacific University on November 9–10, 2001. Those speeches were adapted by their authors for this book.

Library Cataloging Data:

Celebrating Middle-earth: *The Lord of the Rings* as a Defense of Western Civilization

West, Jr., John G. [Garrett], editor (1964–)

Contributors: Janet Blumberg, Kerry Dearborn, Phillip Goggans, Peter Kreeft, Joseph Pearce, and John G. West, Jr.

107 p. 6 x 9 in. (152 x 229 mm)

ISBN: 1-58742-012-0 (alk. paperback)

ISBN: 1-58742-013-9 (alk. hardback)

Library of Congress Control Number: 2002106892

Inkling Books, Seattle, WA Internet: http://www.InklingBooks.com/

Published in the United States of America on acid-free paper.

First Edition, First Printing, June 2002

Dedication

For John and Kathryn Lindskoog, lovers of both Beauty and Truth.

Contents

Preface

John G. West, Jr.

"The book is too original and too opulent for any final judgement on a first reading," declared C. S. Lewis soon after publication of J. R. R. Tolkien's *The Lord of the Rings.* "But we know at once that it has done things to us. We are not quite the same men..."[1] Lewis added that he had "little doubt that the book will soon take its place among the indispensables."

Tolkien was not so sure, worrying that modern readers would find his imaginary history of Middle-earth unappealing. Years later, Tolkien remained astonished that anyone else would find value in what he wrote: "I have never had much confidence in my own work, and even now when I am assured... much to my grateful surprise...that it has value for other people, I feel diffident, reluctant as it were to expose my world of imagination to possibly contemptuous eyes and ears."[2]

Yet it was C. S. Lewis's confidence, not Tolkien's diffidence that proved prophetic, at least as far as the reading public was concerned. Tens of millions of readers found themselves enthralled by *The Lord of the Rings,* making it arguably the most beloved work of twentieth-century English literature. Today millions of additional people are being introduced to Tolkien's tale for the first time through director Peter Jackson's lavish film adaptation of the story.

While the public has heaped praise on Tolkien's work, many critics have been less enthusiastic. Regarding the *The Lord of the Rings* as an exercise in escapism and nostalgia, they treat the story's popular acclaim as proof of its shallowness. The critics' disdain for *The Lord of the Rings* probably has less to do with any actual deficiencies of the story than with the story's underlying point of view. The problem is not that *The Lord of the Rings* lacks a profound message; it is that critics often regard its message as profoundly wrong.

Tolkien was both a devout Christian and a dedicated scholar of Western intellectual and literary traditions, and his love for Christianity and the West stand at the core of his narrative. Far from being simple escapism or blind nostalgia, Tolkien's saga actually confronts many of the idols of modernism and post-modernism. In the face of contemporary moral relativism, *The Lord of the Rings* teaches the existence of an absolute moral law binding on all times and cultures. In the face of scientific materialism, *The Lord of the Rings* gives voice to the transcendent spiritual reality behind ordinary life. In the face of an ever larger (and ever more controlling) welfare state, *The Lord of the Rings* searingly depicts the consequences of absolute power, tyranny and totalitarianism. In an age where art is dominated by cynicism and the anti-hero, *The Lord of the Rings* revives the traditional view that good art is more than mere technique — to be truly admirable, it must somehow extol the good, the true, and the beautiful. Tolkien's saga also supplies insight into the permanent limitations of human nature, and it leads readers back into the riches of the Western artistic tradition by drawing afresh on literary forms and conventions of the past millennium. The purpose of this book is to explore some of the many ways that Tolkien's book may be read as a defense of these rich legacies of Western civilization.

The essays published here began as papers delivered at a conference held at Seattle Pacific University in November of 2001. Titled "Celebrating Middle Earth: *The Lord of the Rings* as a Defense of Western Civilization," the conference was organized by the C. S. Lewis Institute at Seattle Pacific University, a joint project of Seattle Pacific University's Society of Fellows and the Seattle-based Discovery Institute. The conference was co-sponsored by the Intercollegiate Studies Institute, which provided financial support to make the event possible, as did the Earhart Foundation.

Celebrating Middle-earth

Given that there would have been no book without the "Celebrating Middle Earth" conference, I would like to take this opportunity to thank some of the many individuals who made the conference a reality. Sig Swanstrom and Bobbie Taylor of the Society of Fellows deserve special recognition, as do Bruce Chapman, Steve Jost, Doug Bilderback, and the rest of the staff of Discovery Institute. Their encouragement and meticulous attention to detail made the conference a success. Additional thanks should go to Dr. Michael Macdonald, my colleague at Seattle Pacific University who helped establish the C. S. Lewis Institute on our campus in the late 1970s, and Michael Wallacavage of the Intercollegiate Studies Institute, who has faithfully supported the activities of the Lewis Institute through the years.

Just as the original conference would not have become a reality without the above individuals, this book would not have been possible without the support and assistance of Mike Perry of Inkling Books. I gratefully thank him for embracing this project and then bringing it to reality.

Sponsors

C. S. Lewis and Public Life, Discovery Institute
http://www.discovery.org/lewis/
Phone: 206-292-0401
1402 Third Ave. Suite 400, Seattle, WA 98101

Intercollegiate Studies Institute
http://www.isi.org/
Phone: 302-652-4600
P.O. Box 4431, Wilmington, DE 19807

The Society of Fellows, Seattle Pacific University
http://advance.spu.edu/Fellows/Overview.asp
Phone: 206-281-2000
3307 Third Avenue West, Seattle, WA 98119-1997

Endnotes

1 C. S. Lewis, "Tolkien's The Lord of the Rings," in *C. S. Lewis on Stories and Other Essays on Literature,* edited by Walter Hooper (New York: Harcourt Brace Jovanovich, 1982), p. 90.

2 Tolkien to Clyde S. Kilby, December 18, 1965, in *The Letters of J. R. R. Tolkien,* edited by Humphrey Carpenter (Boston: Houghton Mifflin Co., 1981), p. 366.

Contributors

Janet Blumberg is Professor of English (*Emeritus*) at Seattle Pacific University. Her scholarship has focused on Medieval and Renaissance literature.

Kerry Dearborn is Associate Professor of Theology at Seattle Pacific University. She has special interests in the writings of George MacDonald and the Christian imagination.

Phillip Goggans is Associate Professor of Philosophy at Seattle Pacific University. His main scholarly interests are ancient philosophy and natural law theory.

Peter Kreeft is Professor of Philosophy at Boston College and author of more than twenty-five books, including *Back to Virtue, Between Heaven and Hell, Love is Stronger than Death, C.S. Lewis for the Third Millennium,* and *Heaven: The Heart's Deepest Longing.*

Joseph Pearce is Writer-in-Residence at Ave Maria College in Michigan and co-editor of the *St. Austin Review.* He is author of such books as *Tolkien, Man and Myth: A Literary Life, Solzhenitsyn: A Soul in Exile, Wisdom and Innocence: A Life of G.K. Chesterton,* and *Literary Converts.*

John West is Associate Professor of Political Science at Seattle Pacific University and a Senior Fellow at the Seattle-based Discovery Institute. His publications include *The Politics of Revelation and Reason, The C.S. Lewis Readers' Encyclopedia, The Encyclopedia of Religion in American Politics,* and *The Theology of Welfare.*

CHAPTER

1

The Lord of the Rings as a Defense of Western Civilization

John G. West, Jr.

When readers in England a few years ago were asked to name "the greatest book of the century," they chose J. R. R. Tolkien's *The Lord of the Rings*. Many critics were scandalized, finding it incomprehensible that the public could honor a work the literary community had largely dismissed as old-fashioned, didactic, and escapist. Yet the survey was far from a fluke. Tolkien's writings have sold more than 100 million copies worldwide, spawned fan clubs and scholarly organizations, and inspired music and artworks by a number of gifted artists. Now Hollywood is releasing three lavish live-action films based on the saga, and people who have never even read *The Lord of the Rings* are flocking to see it on the screen.

What is so entrancing about Tolkien's work that it inspires such devotion? Why is it still worth reading nearly a half century after its publication?

While there are many possible answers to those questions, I would like to focus on just one: We should read *The Lord of the Rings* because it presents a remarkable defense of Western civilization—a defense in these dark times that we sorely need. I am far from claiming that Tolkien consciously created his work as a defense of the West or as some sort of allegory of current world affairs. Allegory was a form of writing that he disliked.[1] But Tolkien wasn't against what he called "applicability,"[2] and he did not deny that his work could be applicable to many things in the contemporary world. It is in that spirit of "applicability" that Tolkien's work may be read as a defense of Western civilization—that glorious melting pot of Greco-Roman, Judeo-Christian, and pagan Northern European cultures.

In a literary sense, *The Lord of the Rings* might be regarded as a defense of the West by its virtual resurrection of the literary forms and themes from the West's greatest cultures. In an age when writers and artists routinely scorned the wisdom of the past—an age dominated by the anti-heroes of the literary naturalists, the nihilism of the cultural relativists, the purportedly scientific atheism of writers on the brink of suicide—Tolkien's epic arrived like a bracing mountain wind, for it introduced modern readers to forms of literature that are unafraid to explore truth as well as ambiguity, beauty as well as ugliness, good as well as evil, and heroism as well as cowardice. To read Tolkien is to read more than a thousand years of Western literature encapsulated into one tale. C. S. Lewis traced the roots of *The Lord of the Rings* back to *The Odyssey*. Tolkien himself wrote: "I was brought up in the Classics, and first discovered the sensation of literary pleasure in Homer."[3] Tolkien's mythology draws on the Oedipus plays, the Bible, and above all, the Norse sagas.[4] As literary scholar Janet Blumberg has pointed out, Tolkien's epic also draws on Anglo-Saxon and High Medieval writings.[5] Tolkien defends the literature of Western civilization by showing his readers its breathtaking vitality.

In an even more profound sense, however, *The Lord of the Rings* is a defense of Western civilization because of its articulation of four overarching themes that serve as cornerstones for the entire Western tradition.

Natural Law

The first theme is natural law. For more than 2,000 years of Western civilization, the leaders of politics and culture had no difficulty drawing what they thought were objective moral distinctions between good and evil. From Aristotle's *Nicomachean Ethics* to Cicero's *De Republica* to the writings of Paul, Augustine, and Aquinas to the documents of the American Founding, the standard teaching of the West was that we could—and should—make public moral judgments, because there is a universal moral order binding on all human beings.

It was this objective moral order to which our Founding Fathers appealed in the Declaration of Independence when they spoke of the "Laws of Nature and Nature's God" and declared that all men are endowed by their Creator with certain inalienable rights. Indeed, this belief in an objective moral order supplies the basis for the Western belief in universal human rights—rights that are possessed by all people, not just the blessed few in one favored culture. And it is this universal moral law spanning time and culture that permeates Tolkien's saga. Indeed, said C. S. Lewis, it provides "the basis of the whole Tolkienian world."[6] To highlight merely one especially important passage: In *The Two Towers*, the character Aragorn is asked: "How shall a man judge what to do in such times?" And Aragorn replies, "As he ever has judged.... Good and ill have not changed since yesteryear; nor are they one thing among Elves and Dwarves and another among Men."[7]

In other words, good and evil are the same across cultures. There is not one moral standard for Elves and another for Dwarves or men. Tolkien in this dialogue seems to recall a famous passage from Cicero in *De Republica*, where Cicero wrote: "And there will not be different laws at Rome and at Athens, or different laws now and in the future, but one eternal and unchangeable law will be valid for all nations and all times."[8]

We live during a time when many among our cultural elites need to hear Tolkien's clarion defense of natural law. For these people morality is either relative—or worse—an illusion. It is dictated completely by arbitrary cultural preferences or by the non-moral process of survival of the fittest. In the words of sociobiologists E. O. Wilson and Michael Ruse, "Morality... is merely an adaptation put in place to further our reproductive ends.... In an important sense, ethics as we understand it is an illusion fobbed off on us by our genes to get us to cooperate."[9]

Of course, the horrific events of September 11, 2001 seem to have startled even our culture-makers into acknowledging that there are some things that are really evil—at least to a point.

The President of ABC News was asked by journalism students whether he thought the Pentagon had been a "legitimate military target" chosen by the terrorists. He replied that while "perhaps" he might be able to take a position on that question in his "private life," "as a journalist" he felt "strongly" that he "should not be taking a position" on whether the attack on the Pentagon "was right or wrong."[10] To read *The Lord of the Rings* is to be reminded afresh of why such comments are so bankrupt. And this reminder is a ringing affirmation of the best of the Western tradition.

The Fall

A second theme in *The Lord of the Rings* that embodies the Western tradition is the Fall. From the Genesis account of Adam and Eve to Hesiod's tale of Pandora's Box to the works of Madison and Hamilton and the other American Founding Fathers, Western philosophy, politics and literature are shot through with the inevitable imperfection of human beings. "All have sinned and fall short of the glory of God," declared Paul in Romans.[11] "[A]ny man who has power is led to abuse it," said Montesquieu in *The Spirit of the Laws*.[12] "If men were angels, no government would be necessary," added Madison in *Federalist #51*,[13] clearly implying that men are far from angelic. Because of the recognition of the inevitability of human imperfection, there is a profoundly anti-utopian strain in Western political thought.

From the mixed government of Aristotle to the checks and balances of modern constitutionalism, Western political thought has urged the need to balance power against power because no ruler is perfect. "So that one cannot abuse power, power must check power by the arrangement of things," wrote Montesquieu.[14] "Ambition must be made to counteract ambition," echoed Madison.[15]

Western thought also has proclaimed the utter foolishness of believing that human leaders and human institutions can somehow bring about a heaven on earth. In the words of George Washington, "the best Institutions may be abused by human depravity; and... they may even, in some instances, be made subservient to the vilest of purposes."[16]

Celebrating Middle-earth

According to Tolkien, the concept of fall was one of the three great themes in his mythology of Middle-earth. "There cannot be any 'story' without a fall," he wrote, "... at least not for human minds as we know them and have them." Indeed, "all stories are ultimately about the fall."[17] In *The Lord of the Rings*, the utopian attempt to deny the reality of the Fall forms the necessary backdrop to the story, though most readers probably don't realize this fact.

In *The Lord of the Rings*, we meet Sauron already full-grown in his evil. But you will miss Tolkien's point if that is all you know about Sauron, for Sauron was not always evil incarnate. In *The Fellowship of the Ring*, the reader is given a hint of this when Gandalf says, "Nothing is evil in the beginning. Even Sauron was not so."[18] Elsewhere, Tolkien explained how Sauron initially won over many of the Elves by seeking to "reorganize" and "rehabilitate" the lands ruined by the great war against the First Enemy in Middle-earth. Sauron "was still fair in that early time," writes Tolkien, "and his motives and those of the Elves seemed to go partly together: the healing of the desolate lands. Sauron found their weak point in suggesting that, helping one another, they could make Western Middle-earth as beautiful as Valinor. It was really a veiled attack on the gods, an incitement to try and make a separate independent paradise."[19] In other words, Sauron sought to create heaven on earth as a substitute for the real heaven. Thus he appropriated to himself the prerogatives of the gods and becomes "the reincarnation of Evil."[20] Because of the Fall, we cannot create heaven on earth, and if we try, we are more likely to bring forth Hell instead.

Tolkien did not write *The Lord of the Rings* as a commentary on modern totalitarianism, but he certainly recognized that his saga did implicitly critique the utopian claims of both Nazism and Communism—and the claims of inevitable progress made in the name of modern science and technology in democratic countries. Utopianism wears many disguises. It can be the ruthless attempt to impose a universal good by tyranny, but it can also be the stubborn unwillingness to face *necessary* evils—such as war.

The Lord of the Rings does not glorify war, but it does suggest that its profound tragedy may be unavoidable in a fallen world.

When the Warden of the Houses of Healing in Gondor laments to Lady Éowyn that, "the world is full enough of hurts and mischances without wars to multiply them," Eowyn responds tartly: "It needs but one foe to breed a war, not two."[21] Good people cannot stop a war merely by turning the other cheek.

At a more general level, Tolkien in *The Lord of the Rings* challenges the utopian thinking that prevents one from taking sides in a moral controversy because no side is perfect. Far from portraying the conflict between good and evil as a battle between cardboard people who are perfectly good or perfectly evil, *The Lord of the Rings* does a superb job in uncovering the conflicting and even dishonorable motives of those on the "right" side of the controversy—think of Boromir and Denethor. But part of the recognition of the Fall is to realize that despite the fact that no person is wholly good or wholly evil, one is still obliged to fight for on side of justice, even if one's side is tainted by sin and impure motives. "There are... conflicts about important things or ideas," wrote Tolkien. "In such cases I am more impressed by the extreme importance of being on the right side, than I am disturbed by the revelation of the jungle of confused motives, private purposes, and individual actions (noble or base) in which the *right* and the *wrong* in actual human conflicts are commonly involved."[22]

This does not mean that Tolkien thought we should be blind to the evils on our own side as long as our cause is just. In fact, *The Lord of the Rings* powerfully warns those fighting on the right side about the dangers to their own souls, particularly the dangers posed by blind vengeance. For all the warfare in *The Lord of the Rings*, Tolkien's epic is far more about mercy than vengeance—mercy to Gollum, mercy to Saruman, mercy to the Quisling Hobbits in the Shire at the end of the story. Recall how Frodo commands in "The Scouring of the Shire" that there be no killing of fellow Hobbits even as the tyranny is overthrown. Recall how both Frodo and Gandalf are against killing Gollum. It is not so much that Gollum, or Saruman, or disloyal Hobbits don't deserve death. They do. It is what the taking of their lives in vengeance will do to the victors that Tolkien is concerned about. Here Tolkien is at his most Christian in appreciating that none of us is so good that he cannot fall, and that vengeance even in a righteous cause is so overpowering that it will destroy us—and will only lead to further cycles of violence. One need only think of the seemingly intractable hatreds in places like Bosnia, Northern Ireland, and the Middle East to understand the truth of Tolkien's insight.

While Tolkien insisted that *The Lord of the Rings* was not about World War II, it is certainly true that its theme of the need for mercy even during wartime had a real world parallel. Even as Tolkien worked on his epic, he wrote his son Christopher about an article in the local newspaper that seriously advocated the systematic extermination "of the entire German nation as the only proper course after military victory: because, if you please, they are rattlesnakes, and don't know the difference between good and evil!" "What of the writer?" mused Tolkien. "You can't fight the Enemy with his own Ring without turning into an Enemy," he concluded, "but unfortunately Gandalf's wisdom seems long ago to have passed with him into the True West."[23]

Actually, Gandalf's wisdom had not quite departed Middle-earth, for after World War II the Western allies did a truly remarkable thing in the history of the world—rather than take vengeance on the countries they vanquished, they rebuilt them, turning foes into friends. Gandalf's wisdom could be seen again in 2001, as the West sent thousands of tons of food to the Afghanistan people even as it rooted out the Taliban.

Yet Tolkien's warnings about the universality of the Fall—and how it touches every part of our lives—is something we still need to hear today.

Freedom

A third theme that can be found in Tolkien's saga is freedom. Freedom or liberty is surely one of the cardinal principles of Western civilization: it underlies much of Western literature, politics, philosophy, and religion. It is so central to the West's self-understanding that it is often debased and misused by pro-pagandists, a fact which Tolkien lamented. Yet the cheap rhetoric of demagogues does not diminish the power of authentic freedom. While that authentic freedom is comprised of many parts, I will highlight two. The first is moral freedom—the idea that we are not merely cogs in a cosmic machine of fate, but that we are called to make genuine moral choices, and we are therefore morally accountable for our choices. This is not to deny that there are powerful forces that impinge on our choices, but it is to maintain that even in the midst of the forces that act on us we have genuine moments of moral freedom, and those moments are critical for determining our individual destinies.

This idea of genuine moral freedom is at the heart of the traditional western legal system, and it is also at the core of such great works of the West as Dante's *Divine Comedy*. In Canto 16 of the *Purgatorio*, Dante writes that "your Free Will... though it may grow faint in its first struggles with the heavens, can still surmount all obstacles if nurtured well. You are subjects of a greater power, a nobler nature that creates your mind, and over this the spheres have no control."[24] In *The Lord of the Rings*, Frodo, Gollum, Denethor and others all experience moments of genuine moral freedom. At the end of *The Fellowship of the Ring*, Tolkien provides a particularly compelling account of one such moment during a struggle within Frodo on the summit of Amon Hen: "[T]wo powers strove in him. For a moment, perfectly balanced between their piercing points, he writhed, tormented. Suddenly he was aware of himself again. Frodo, neither the Voice nor the Eye: free to choose, and with one remaining instant in which to do so. He took the Ring off his finger."[25] Time and again, the characters in *The Lord of the Rings* remind us that we are given the opportunity to make genuine choices and we are morally accountable for them.

A second type of freedom central to the West is political and social—the right to live one's life in accord with the moral law free from micromanagement by either one's neighbors or one's rulers. "Countries are well cultivated, not as they are fertile but as they are free," wrote Montesquieu.[26] "[T]he mass of mankind has not been born with saddles on their backs, nor a favored few booted and spurred, ready to ride legitimately, by the grace of God," declared Jefferson.[27]

The freedom to be left alone—especially the freedom of ordinary people to be left alone by the elites who want to rule them for their own good—is a central theme in *The Lord of the Rings*. It is shown perhaps most clearly by the Hobbits, most of whom

Celebrating Middle-earth

are perfectly willing to live their quiet, boring, and mundane lives without any interference from officious busybodies, thank you. Tolkien's heart was clearly in the Shire, and he even called himself a Hobbit on occasion.[28] But even outside the Shire, one gets the idea that to be left alone to rule one's own family and community was prized. In *The Two Towers*, Éomer of Rohan declares to Aragorn: "We desire only to be free, and to live as we have lived, keeping our own, and serving no foreign lord."[29] And the Company of Nine itself was supposed to represent all of what Tolkien called the "Free Peoples"—Dwarves, Men, Elves, and Hobbits—those who lived in the freedom of self-rule rather than under the slavery of Sauron's totalitarianism. They fought to maintain their freedoms, not to set up a new universal empire.

True, the story ends with the ascendancy of a King, but this is a King who believes in self-government, not absolute rule from the top down. Revisiting the village of Bree near the end of the book, Gandalf engages in a discussion with Mr. Butterbur of *The Prancing Pony*. When Gandalf informs Butterbur that there is a new King and the old highway will be reopened, Butterbur shakes his head and says, "We want to be let alone." "You will be let alone," replies Gandalf. As they continue their discussion, Butterbur accepts that the new developments "will be good for business, no doubt. So long as [the King] lets Bree alone." "He will," says Gandalf again. "He knows [Bree] and loves it."[30] The new King will not be a meddler.

The Lord of the Rings thus embodies Tolkien's passionate belief in a limited government that does not overmanage the lives of citizens. In the midst of writing *The Lord of the Rings*, Tolkien wrote whimsically to his son Christopher, then 18, and in the RAF:

> My political opinions lean more and more to Anarchy (philosophically understood, meaning abolition of control not whiskered men with bombs)—or to 'unconstitutional' Monarchy. I would arrest anybody who uses the word State… and after a chance of recantation, execute them if they remained obstinate! Government is an abstract noun meaning the art and process of governing and it should be an offence to write it with a capital G…. Anyway, the proper study of Man is anything but Man; and the most

improper job of any man, even saints... is bossing other men. Not one in a million is fit for it, and least of all those who seek the opportunity.... Give me a king whose chief interest in life is stamps, railways, or race-horses....[31]

Tolkien believed that governments should operate with strictly limited objectives because he thought that this would safeguard *genuine* cultural diversity. Bureaucratic centralization—national standards applied from the top down—was deadly in his view. In another letter to his son, Tolkien expressed his fears of the world centralization that might follow even if England won World War II:

The bigger things get the smaller and duller or flatter the globe gets. It is getting to be all one blasted little provincial suburb. When they have introduced American sanitation, morale-pep, feminism, and mass production throughout the Near East, Middle East, Far East, USSR, the Pampas... the Danubian Basin, Equatorial Africa, Hither Further and Inner Mumbo-land... and the villages of the darkest Berk-shire, how happy we shall be. At any rate it ought to cut down travel. There will be nowhere to go.[32]

One can only wonder what Tolkien would have thought of the European Union and its growing battalions of bureaucratic planners! Tolkien's articulation of the reasons for freedom defends Western civilization by warning us of the dangers in our midst of nationalized planning, cultural homogenization, and rule by hordes of state experts who give us endless instructions on what we ought to do.

The Transcendent

A fourth theme that can be found in *The Lord of the Rings* is a sense of the transcendent, an acknowledgment that the material universe is not the sum total of reality, and that human beings are not—and never will be—the rulers of the cosmic order. While the understanding of the transcendent reaches its most sublime pitch within the Judeo-Christian tradition, it can also be found in Platonic idealism and Aristotle's *Metaphysics*, as well as in the pagan religions of Northern Europe. Throughout Western history, the transcendent has manifested itself in many ways and many forms. It is at the root of the notion of a higher law binding on all human cultures. It is the source of the maxim that "man has no right to play God." It is the foundation for doctrines of Providence and Fate, the idea that human beings are not ultimately in control of the history of the universe. At a more practical level, a sense of the transcendent provides another justification for limited government—because it recognizes that man is not God and therefore has no right to rule in the place of God. It supplies another reason to be anti-utopian, because even if we were morally perfect (which we are not), we would still be finite. We are not omniscient, and we cannot see with clarity into the future; therefore if we try to act as if we are omniscient, we will botch things horribly. In the words of Hawthorne, "no human effort, on a grand scale, has ever yet resulted according to the purpose of its projectors.... We miss the good we sought, and do the good we little cared for."[33] Finally, a sense of the transcendent is the inspiration for the belief that man is made for more than bread alone—the belief that the fundamental realities are spiritual rather than physical.

The transcendent has always had its detractors in the West, of course. In the ancient and medieval worlds, it was opposed by those who sought to invest their human rulers with divinity, or at the least with the authority of the divine. Clothed with absolute powers, such rulers could not be expected to follow the limitations of ordinary human beings. By making men gods they denied the reality of the true God. Today, however, the chief enemy of the transcendent is Scientific Materialism—the assertion that all we are and all we believe can be reduced to matter in motion. A corollary to this claim is the belief that once we understand the forces that shape matter, we can reshape the world to our liking. Tolkien identified scientific materialism as one of the embodiments of the "evil spirit" in the modern world.[34] By reducing all things to matter in motion, it denies the transcendent and its spiritual realities outright. And by claiming that we can discover scientific laws that will allow us to reshape human destiny, it promotes an unrelenting utopianism that has left devastation in its path. In the past, it inspired crude efforts in eugenics through forced sterilization, barbaric experiments with techniques like lobotomies to eliminate anti-social behavior, and even Hitler's pseudo-scientific "final solution." In the future, who knows? We can look forward to the expanding frontiers of bioengineering—unrestrained by the maxim "man has no right to play God," because God isn't supposed to exist.

According to Tolkien, the conflict in *The Lord of the Rings* in its most fundamental sense is over this denial of the transcendent. "It is about God, and His sole right to divine honour," he wrote. "The Eldar and the Númenoreans believed in The One, the true God, and held worship of any other person an abomination. Sauron desired to be a God-King, and was held to be this by his servants."[35]

The Lord of the Rings defends the transcendent by exposing the utter bankruptcy of any attempt to replace God with anyone or anything else. It likewise opens the door to the transcendent by continually emphasizing the finiteness of created beings and their lack of omniscience. Even Gandalf cannot see the future exhaustively. "For even the very wise cannot see all ends," he tells Frodo in *The Fellowship of the Rings*.[36] It is a saying that keeps popping up in the story, as does the sense that there is much more to the story than Tolkien is able to tell us. The characters are free to make genuine choices, to be sure, but do those choices alone dictate the history of Middle-earth? Perhaps not. Early on, Gandalf lets Frodo know just how incredible it was that his friend Bilbo happened upon the One Ring. "Behind that," he says, "there was something else at work, beyond any design of the Ring-maker. I can put it no plainer than by saying that Bilbo was meant to find the Ring, and not by its maker. In which case you also were meant to have it. And that may be an encouraging thought."[37] "It is not!" protests Frodo, but for the reader, it really is an encouraging thought—if nonetheless a mysterious one. As the plot moves along, the mystery deepens, for everything does not seem to happen just by chance or necessity. Could it be design? *The Lord of the Rings* does not give us a final answer, but it certainly raises the question in the minds of thoughtful readers. And by raising the question of whether there is some intelligence other than ourselves who is moving history, Tolkien nudges us to think about whether this may also be the case in our own lives.

I have suggested that Tolkien's *The Lord of the Rings* can be read as a defense of Western civilization, but by now it should be clear that it is also a critique of certain trends that have come to dominate the West during the past century. So to say that *The Lord of the Rings* is a defense of Western civilization is not to say that it is a defense of our civilization as it exists. Instead, it has much to tell us about the disrepair into which Western civilization has fallen. As Tolkien would sometimes write, we face "Mordor in our midst."[38] Since September 11, 2001 it is easier for most of us to believe that. Lest we have any doubts, we can see the poisonous fruit produced by the forces of Mordor in the rubble of the World Trade Center.

But what should be our response to Mordor in our midst?

I think Tolkien's epic provides guidance. Certainly part of our response should be support for the military efforts currently underway. *We* did not seek war; war was declared on *us*, and now we must respond. However, *The Lord of the Rings* suggests that the terrorists are far from our only danger. During wartime, we must of course look to the enemy without—but we must also look to the enemy within ourselves. For in a fallen world, even those fighting a righteous cause can face temptations destructive of their souls. Two of the main temptations are embodied in Tolkien's story by Saruman and Denethor.

Saruman the White was the greatest wizard of Middle-earth. He had been a tremendous force for good, and he knew it. His achievements made him proud, and in his pride he overestimated both his knowledge and his power. He came to think that he could defeat Sauron by using Sauron's methods. He optimistically believed that he could take Sauron's place and rule the world for its own good. In other words, he aspired to God-like power just as Sauron had. He blasphemed against the transcendent by denying that there were any limits that we was obliged to follow. In the end, his optimism was shown to be foolish. He was not as omniscient as he had thought; and had he been, he would merely would have become another Sauron. Saruman is a warning to those who are so certain we will win over our enemies because of our superior wisdom and strength. After all, aren't we the world's leader in technology? Don't we have the most firepower? Isn't our economy still the strongest in the world? Saruman is also a warning to those who are willing to win at all costs—the end justifies any means. Following that road, we may in fact win, but only at the price of becoming our enemies.

Denethor's temptation is also borne of pride. He is certain that he sees the future as well, but that vision feeds despair, not optimism. Denethor becomes convinced that resistance is futile because the future has already been decided. He usurps the role of God just as much as Saruman does, both because he refuses to leave room for God to act in history, and because he claims the type of omniscience that only God can have of the future. Denethor is deluded into denying his own finite knowledge of the world, and this denial leads him into madness and annihilation on the very eve of victory.

In their own ways, both Denethor and Saruman denied the transcendent—to their own destruction. Together they illustrate what C. S. Lewis thought was the underlying moral of *The Lord of the Rings*: to "recall [us] from facile optimism and wailing pessimism alike, to that hard, yet not quite desperate, insight into Man's unchanging predicament by which heroic ages have lived."

That moral is especially appropriate for us today. We do not know what tomorrow will bring. Bio-terrorism, chemical attacks, nuclear annihilation. We do not know how many hundreds—or thousands—will die in the years ahead. Tolkien's *The Lord of the Rings* reminds us that it is not in our power either to know or to command what will happen in the future. All we are responsible for is to go about our appointed tasks with as much wisdom and justice and courage as we can muster.

"Let us have faith that right makes might, and in that faith, let us, to the end, dare to do our duty as we understand it."[39] So declared Abraham Lincoln on the eve of the American Civil War. We can fortify his words with the hope of Gandalf that "there [is] something else at work [in history], beyond any design of" of latter-day Saurons.[40] And if we wish, we can add to that the comfort of Galadriel who tells Frodo and his companions, "Do not let your hearts be troubled"[41]—for we know someone else who says those words, and His word is true.[42]

Endnotes

1 "I cordially dislike allegory in all its manifestations...." Foreword, J. R. R. Tolkien, *The Fellowship of the Rings* (New York: Ballantine Books, 1965), p. xi.

2 Ibid.

3 Tolkien to Robert Murray, December 2, 1953 in *The Letters of J. R. R. Tolkien* (Boston: Houghton Mifflin, 1981), p. 172. Henceforth *Letters.*

4 See Tolkien to Milton Waldman in *Letters,* p. 150.

5 See Janet Blumberg, "The Literary Background of *The Lord of the Rings,*" *Celebrating Middle-earth* (Seattle: Inkling, 2002).

6 C. S. Lewis, "Tolkien's *The Lord of the Rings,*" ed. Walter Hooper, *On Stories and Other Essays on Literature* (New York: Harcourt Brace Jovanovich, 1982), p. 87.

7 J. R. R. Tolkien, *The Two Towers* (New York: Ballantine Books, 1965), Bk. III, Ch. 2, p. 50.

8 Cicero, *De Republica* (Cambridge: Harvard University Press, 1927), Bk. III, Ch. xxii, p. 211. [Vol. XVI of Loeb Classical Library volumes of Cicero.]

9 Michael Ruse and E. O. Wilson, "The Evolution of Ethics," in James Hutchingson, *Religion and the Natural Sciences: The Range of Engagement* (San Diego: Harcourt Brace Jovanovich College Publishers, 1993), p. 310.

10 "Media Leadership in Our Time," *The Weekly Standard,* November 12, 2001, p. 44. The President of ABC News eventually retracted these remarks due to the firestorm of protest they provoked.

11 Romans 3:23.

12 Montesquieu, *The Spirit of the Laws,* ed. Anne Cohler, Basia Miller, and Harold Stone, (New York: Cambridge University Press, 1989), Bk.11, ch. 4, p. 155.

13 James Madison, Federalist Paper #51 in Alexander Hamilton, James Madison, John Jay, *The Federalist Papers* (New York: New American Library, 1961), p. 322.

14 Montesquieu, *Laws,* Bk. 11, Ch. 4, p. 155.

15 Madison, Federalist #51, *Federalist Papers,* p. 322.

16 George Washington, "[Proposed Address to Congress]," in John C. Fitzpatrick, editor, *The Writings of George Washington from the Original Manuscript Sources,* 1745–1799 (Washington, D.C.: United States George Washington Bicentennial Commission), Vol. 30, pp. 301–302.

17 Tolkien to Milton Waldman, *Letters,* p. 147.

18 *Fellowship of the Ring,* Bk. II, Ch. 2, p. 351.

19 Tolkien to Milton Waldman, *Letters,* p. 152.

20 Ibid., p. 151.

21 J. R. R. Tolkien, *The Return of the King* (New York: Ballantine Books, 1965), Bk. VI, Ch. 5, p. 292.

22 Tolkien, "Notes on W. H. Auden's review of *The Return of the King,*" in *Letters,* p. 242.

23 Tolkien to Christopher Tolkien, September 23–25, 1944, *Letters,* pp. 93–94.

24 Dante, *Purgatory* in Mark Musa, editor, *The Portable Dante,* Canto XVI, lines 76–81.

25 *Fellowship of the Ring*, Bk. II, Ch. 10, p. 519.

26 Montesquieu, *Laws*, Bk. XVIII, Ch. 3.

27 Jefferson to Roger Weightman, June 24, 1826 in Thomas Jefferson, *Writings* (New York: Library of America, 1984), p. 1517.

28 "I am in fact a *Hobbit*." Tolkien to Deborah Webster, October 25, 1958, *Letters*, p. 288.

29 *Two Towers*, Bk. III, Ch. 2, p. 43.

30 *Return of the King*, Bk. VI, Ch. 7, p. 337.

31 Tolkien to Christopher Tolkien, November 29, 1943, *Letters*, pp. 63–64.

32 Tolkien to Christopher Tolkien, December 9, 1943, *Letters*, p. 65.

33 Nathaniel Hawthorne, "Chiefly about War Matters," in *The Writings of Nathaniel Hawthorne* (Boston: Houghton, Mifflin and Company, 1900), Vol. XVII, p. 403.

34 Tolkien to Christopher Tolkien, January 30, 1945, *Letters*, p. 110.

35 "Notes on Auden's Review," *Letters*, p. 243.

36 *Fellowship of the Ring*, Bk. I, Ch. 2, p. 93.

37 Ibid., p. 88.

38 Tolkien to Rayner Unwin, August 29, 1952, *Letters*, p. 165.

39 Abraham Lincoln, "Cooper Institute Address," February 27, 1860 in *Abraham Lincoln: Speeches and Writings, 1859–1865* (New York: Library of America, 1989), p. 130.

40 *Fellowship of the Ring*, Bk. II, Ch. 7, p. 462.

41 Ibid., Bk. I, Ch. 2, p. 88.

42 "Let not your heart be troubled," John 14:1.

2

Wartime Wisdom

Ten Uncommon Insights about Evil in *The Lord of the Rings*

Peter Kreeft

Evil.

For almost half a century our culture has been embarrassed at words like "wickedness," "sin," "judgment," "punishment," and "Hell," like a teenager embarrassed at being seen with her parents in a mall.

Some of our Deep Thinkers say evil is a temporary stage of evolution, a hangover from ancient barbarisms, or provincialisms of race, class and gender that we will just grow out of as we grow out of diapers.

Others say evil is ignorance, thus curable by education. We are still waiting for the cure to take.

A study of which Nazis were the most willing to kill Jews in the death camps showed that this willingness was indeed related to education but not in the way expected: the most educated they were, the more they were willing. The same is true now about approval of America's death camps for unborn babies. (By the way, RU-486 is being manufactured by a derivative of the same company that manufactured Zyklon-B, Roussel-Uclaf, a subsidiary of Hoechst, which was a spinoff of I. G. Farben. Divine providence is darkly ironic.)

Some say that evil against others is only the acting out of a lack of positive self-esteem; that Hitler was not *enough* in love with himself.

Some are more philosophically sophisticated and realize that evil is not a thing or a substance, as the Manichees thought, but disordered good. They often rush from this insight to the illogical but comforting conclusion that evil is not really real and not, therefore, really terrible, for it is only a lack of perfection.

Most of us (who are not nihilists, neo-Nazis, or pseudo-Islamic terrorists) believe that good is stronger than evil and therefore that evil is less mighty and terrible than good. We tend to conclude from this (also illogically) that we fear it too much, not too little. We even admire FDR's famous nonsense that "we have nothing to fear but fear itself." This strikes us as somehow psychologically healthy and even pious, and its denial unhealthy and even impious.

But then we saw the spectacular evils of September 11, 2001. In the chorus of voices that filled our media for the next two months, one voice was conspicuously silent from the babble: psychobabble. What became of our prophets, the pop psychologists? Where have all the gurus gone? They went where dreams go when the alarm clock goes off, when our Towers of Babble crashed to the ground.

We have seen the limitations of "the power of positive thinking," Norman Vincent Peale's religious version of pop psychology. We used to find Peale appealing and St. Paul appalling for his "negativism" and "judgmentalism" and "polemics." Now we're beginning to find Peale appalling and Paul appealing.

Now we are able to see the movie version of the book that everyone *but* our experts, the critics, chose as the greatest book of the twentieth century. (Of course, some truths are so obvious that only experts can deny them.) The timing of this movie is a patently Providential coincidence, for this movie is a story about evil. We need this story because we have been overgrown adolescents playing with paper airplanes and catching butterflies, and then suddenly our airplanes caught fire and our butterflies caught anthrax. We need this story because we need a wizard like Gandalf or Tolkien to remind us of forgotten wisdom. We need this story because when we have embraced a hundred heresies as the orthodoxy of the future, *The Lord of the Rings* offers us the only possible radicalism left: tradition.

Some say there are only twelve basic plots, some say seven, and some say three. I say one: jihad, spiritual warfare between good and evil in some form. Every story worth telling has three stages: a situation is first set up, then upset, then reset, either happily or unhappily. First there is good, then evil, then warfare, with some resolution (always some, never none, never all). Theologians know this threefold scheme of the greatest story ever told as Creation, Fall, and Redemption. Bilbo called it "There and Back Again"—home, the Road away from home, and the Road back home again. For Frodo, it is the Shire, Mordor, and the Shire (or rather, the Grey Havens).

My purpose here is not to throw some philosophical abstractions onto Tolkien's text to muffle it like snow on a bell, but to let that text ring, to do some bell-ringing in the temple of Tolkien; to call your attention, like a tour guide, to some of his great words that remind us of forgotten wisdom about evil and how to fight it.

My primary purpose is philosophical rather than literary. This sets me at cross purposes (or, better, angled purposes) with Tolkien, for he told us in his Foreword, that his "prime motive was the desire of a tale-teller to try his hand at a really long story that would hold the attention of readers, amuse them, delight them, and at times maybe excite them or deeply move them."[1] So I enter Tolkien's literary store as a thief because I think his words also have great selling power in another store, philosophy. I believe that both literature and philosophy can be legitimate as ends or as means. When Tolkien created his story he used his philosophy (Christianity) as a means to grow the story; I now use his literature as a means to grow some philosophy.

The ten forgotten points of wisdom are:

- That we are at war, not at peace; that our enemy, evil, is real;

- That evil is very big; in fact, immortal;

- That knowing the difference between good and evil is very easy and clear;

- That knowledge is not always a good;

- That what defeats evil is evil itself;
- That evil works for good; and that four of the most powerful weapons against it are:
  - Sacrifice,
  - Humility,
  - Friendship,
  - Words.

1. Evil is Real

Think of the first time you saw the spectacular images on your TV screen September 11, 2001. Now remember not the images but the feelings; not the change outside you but the change inside you. It was a very sharp and clear change because it was so sudden. It was the change from a "peacetime consciousness" to a "wartime consciousness." It was a little like the change from sleeping consciousness to waking consciousness which your alarm clock triggers in you each morning. In fact, it was a lot like that: a sudden light, a sudden enlightenment. The world you woke up to was not brought into being by your act of waking up—it was always there. But *you* were not always "there." If you were dreaming that you were a soldier, you did not cease to be a soldier and begin to be a professor when you woke. You were a professor even while you were dreaming you were a soldier.

Now imagine that instead of a professor dreaming that you were a soldier, you were a soldier dreaming you were a professor. And suppose the dream went on during the day rather than the night. And then and alarm rang. For many of us, that alarm was September 11th. For others, it was a phone call at 3 a.m. about a family emergency or a death. For others, it was the Bible. But we who believe the Bible constantly fall asleep during battle and dream that we are not at war but at peace; that we are in Upper Eden, not Middle-earth, and there is no snake.

There are two philosophies of life. One says "Woe unto him who cries 'Peace! Peace!' When there is no peace." The other says "Woe unto him who cries 'Snake! Snake!' when there is no snake." Which one is the dream and which is the reality?

Before September 11th, most of us saw America as the Hobbits saw the Shire: "a district of well-ordered business; and there in that pleasant corner of the world they plied their well-ordered business of living, and they heeded less and less the world outside where dark things moved, until they came to think that peace and plenty were the rule in Middle-earth and the right of all sensible folk. They forgot or ignored what little they had ever known of the Guardians, and of the labours of those that made possible the long peace of the Shire. They were, in fact, sheltered, but they had ceased to remember it."[2]

Who are our Guardians? Not the CIA or the FBI. We are sheltered not by guardian agents but by guardian angels. And it is good to know just a little about them: not too much, and not nothing, but precisely those glimpses God has in fact given us.

"Dear me! We Tooks and Brandybucks, we can't live long on the heights."

"No," said Merry. "I can't. Not yet, at any rate. But at least, Pippin, we can now see them, and honour them. It is best to love first what you are fitted to love, I suppose: you must start somewhere and have some roots, and the soil of the Shire is deep. Still, there are things deeper and higher; and not a gaffer could tend his garden in what he calls peace but for them, whether he knows about them or not. I am glad I know about them a little."[3]

And so are we. We thank both authors of *The Lord of the Rings*, the inspired one and the Inspiring One, for pulling aside our curtain just a little.

One of the many reasons we voted this book the greatest of the century (in three separate polls), and why the movie will probably be the greatest and most successful movie of all time, is the need for it. That is not why Tolkien wrote it, but is probably one of the reasons why God did. (Of course it's inspired; it's got His fingerprints all over it.) It is a long and beautiful alarm clock.

Our war did not begin in Manhattan but in Eden. Our enemies are not merely terrorists of the body but terrorists of the spirit, "principalities and powers." They come not from Afghanistan but from Hell. You do not need to commit the sin of allegory to see who the Black Riders are.

"'They come from Mordor,' said Strider in a low voice. 'From Mordor, Barliman, if that means anything to you.'"[4]

Strider's suggestively laconic "Do you wish them to find you? They are terrible!"[5] recalls Ingmar Bergman's description of the Angel of Death in "The Seventh Seal": "It's the Angel of Death passing over us, Mia, the Angel of death. And he's *very big.*"

More evils come from Mordor than we know: "Saruman had slowly shaped [Isengard] to his shifting purposes, and made it better, as he thought, being deceived—for all those arts and subtle devices for which he forsook his former wisdom, and which fondly he imagined were his own, came from Mordor."[6]

So did the little local evils in the Shire that had to be "scoured":

"This is worse than Mordor!" said Sam. "Much worse in a way. It comes home to you, as they say, because it is home, and you remember it before it was all ruined."

"Yes, this is Mordor," said Frodo. "Just one of its works."[7]

. . . .

"The very end of the war, I hope," said Merry.

"I hope so," said Frodo and sighed. "The very last stroke. But to think that it should fall here, at the very door of Bag End! Among all my hopes and fears at least I never expected that."[8]

The Great War begins and ends in your house.

2. Evil is Formidable

Our second surprise, after remembering we are at war, is the size of our enemy. We are shocked to hear these words from Gandalf after he returns from death: "War is upon us and all our friends, a war in which only the use of the Ring could give us surety of victory. It fills me with great sorrow and great fear: for much shall be destroyed and all may be lost. I am Gandalf, Gandalf the White, but Black is mightier still."[9]

Later, Gandalf says, after the great battle of the Pelennor Fields:

"My lords, listen to the words of the Steward of Gondor before he died: 'You may triumph on the fields of the

Pelennor for a day, but against the Power that has now arisen there is no victory.' I do not bid you despair, as he did, but to ponder the truth in those words.

"The Stones of Seeing do not lie, and not even the Lord of Barad-dur can make them do so. He can, maybe, by his will choose what things shall be seen by weaker minds, or cause them to mistake the meaning of what they see. Nonetheless it cannot be doubted that when Denethor saw great forces arrayed against him in Mordor, and still more being gathered, he saw that which truly... Victory cannot be achieved by arms... I still hope for victory, but not by arms."[10]

Evil is, in fact, immortal. All our victories against it in this world are temporary: "The evil of Sauron cannot be wholly cured, nor made as if it had not been."[11] "Other evils there are that may come; for Sauron is himself but a servant or emissary."[12] We, like Ransom in *Perelandra,* can only defeat the bodily forms that Evil uses, the Un-men or Nazgûls or evil wizards. We can break the swords but not the Swordsman. Only One can bruise the Swordsman's head, and only by being bruised in His heel.

How can a good defeat evil if not by strength of arms? By embracing weakness, by embracing His heel; by self-sacrifice and humility and suffering and death. Evil is limited to power; it cannot use weakness. It is limited to pride; it cannot use humility. It is limited to inflicting suffering and death; it cannot use suffering and death. It is limited to selfishness; it cannot use selflessness.

Gandalf the White triumphs over Sauron even though "Black is mightier still" because "nothing is evil in the beginning."[13] Evil cannot create or give birth, it can only destroy and give death. For instance, "Trolls are only counterfeits, made by the Enemy in the Great Darkness, in mockery of Ents, as Orcs were of Elves."[14] "The Shadow that bred them can only mock, it cannot make."[15]

That is why one of the lowest and least divine arts is satire, the art of mockery, and why one of the highest and most "subcreative" arts is fantasy. There is no satire but much fantasy in *The Lord of the Rings.* Tolkien says "Let there be Hobbits!" and there are Hobbits. We are back near the Beginning. And nothing is evil in the beginning. Tolkien is not only Gandalf but also

Bombadil; not only Treebeard but also Sam. He is not only old and wise but also young and innocent. He is a child and an old man at once, like the blessed dead when perceived by the living. It takes a child to feel the weight and size of both good and evil. And good as well as evil has a weight in *The Lord of the Rings* that surpasses any other book of the twentieth century. What other twentieth century author could have written a passage like this one? In the midst of Mordor's landscape of death, Sam:

> to keep himself awake, crawled from the hiding place and looked out.... There, peeping among the cloud-wrack above a dark tor high up in the mountains, Sam saw a white star twinkle for a while. The beauty of it smote his heart, as he looked up out of the forsaken land, and hope returned to him. For like a shaft, clear and cold, the thought pierced him that in the end the Shadow was only a small and passing thing: there was light and high beauty for ever beyond its reach.[16]

"Only a small and passing thing"! But this Shadow is Satan, the one who succeeded in killing God for three days. Who but a Christian could ever plumb the depths of evil, and therefore, by hard-won right, of good? (That hard-won right, by the way, is the point of Chesterton's *The Man Who Was Thursday*.) I think of Corrie Ten Boom's shattering statement in the film version of *The Hiding Place*, from the antechambers of Hitler's Mordor in Ravensbruck: "This darkness is very deep, but our God has gone far deeper." When you have been to Calvary, even Ravensbruck looks trivial.

3. Evil is Clear

A third surprise is that the line between good and evil is usually very clear and very obvious. Moses, Confucius, Jesus, and Mohammed all taught this "simplistic" vision and they founded the four most lasting moral regimes in history on it. But our culture is the first one in human history whose experts and teachers have sold their moral birthright for a mess of relativism.

Morality is not hard to know. It is hard to do. It is hard to know only for the clever, for only if you are clever can you invent so many cover-ups that you can make it hard to know. Only the good-hearted see the good, and only the pure-hearted see God. Discernment is not a mental problem but a moral problem. "If your will were to do the will of the Father, you would understand my teaching."[17]

> Said Éomer, "It is hard to be sure of anything among so many marvels. The world is all grown strange. Elf and Dwarf in company walk in our daily fields, and folk speak with the Lady of the Wood and yet live; and the Sword comes back to war that was broken in the long ages ere the fathers of our fathers rode into the Mark! How shall a man judge what to do in such times?"
>
> "As he has ever judged," said Aragorn. "Good and evil have not changed since yesteryear; nor are they one thing among Elves and Dwarves and another among Men. It is a man's part to discern them, as much in the Golden Wood as in his own house."[18]

Aragorn's answer rings like a clear bell in a foggy swamp.

4. Knowledge Is Not Always Good

Another surprise to us is that it is sometimes "better not to know,"[19] as Merry wisely says of the Eucharist-like waybread or *lembas*. (For the folly of wanting to know too much and believe too little about that *lembas*, the Church was split.)

The sacramental, operative words that set in motion the only power that can conquer Sauron are Frodo's fateful, "I will take the Ring, though I do not know the way."[20] (That was Socrates' claim to wisdom too: that he knew that he did *not* know.)

"It is perilous to study too deeply the arts of the Enemy,"[21] as Denethor, like King Saul, discovered at the price of his own soul. Like Eve, Denethor "looked in the Stone and was deceived." We all have such a stone. For Eve it was a fruit; for you or me it is a thought, a first greedy or lustful or proud or despairing thought that is not taken captive to obey Christ.[22]

Denethor and Théoden move in opposite directions, as do the syllables in their names. Denethor moves from life to death because he demands knowledge from the *palantir* before acting. Théoden moves from death to life because he repudiates his tempting *palantir*, Grima Wormtongue (we all have one of those), and takes Gandalf's advice: "To cast aside regret and fear. To do the deed at hand." (Another bell!)

Thought lives in the past of regrets and in the future of fears. Choice and action live in the present of "the deed at hand." Almost never is our moral problem of knowing what to do; almost always, our problem is doing it. William Law says, in *A Serious Call*, "If you will be honest with yourself, you must confess that there is only one reason why you are not as saintly as the primitive Christians (the martyrs): you do not wholly want to be."

We rightly want to look before we leap physically. But we must leap before we look spiritually. "If you do not believe, you will not understand."[23] Faith and works of love cannot wait for knowledge; knowledge must wait for them. We cannot see God, or good, before we are pure of heart because the heart is the very eye with which we see God.

Bilbo's foolish words reverse this order when he expresses to Gandalf has reluctance to leave the Ring behind: "Now (that) it comes to it, I don't like parting with it at all. And I don't really see why I should."[24]

Sometimes, in order to see we must rest our eyes.

5. Evil Defeats Itself

We cannot defeat evil, but we can help it to defeat itself, by a kind of spiritual judo. That's how Christ defeated Satan on Calvary. It was like a Mohammed Ali "Come on and get me" move.

The Ring, says Gandalf, "cannot be unmade by your hands or mine."[25] Even God did what Frodo did to conquer evil for us: "To walk into peril—to Mordor. We must send the Ring to the Fire."[26] Like Orpheus, God went down to Hell for His beloved Euridyce (us) when He cried, "My God, my God, why hast Thou forsaken Me?"

This is the logic of evil. Like a self-contradictory proposition, you cannot refute it with any other proposition, but it refutes itself.

But we must be the bait, as Christ was. The whole Fellowship, in different ways, does this: Gollum does it, unwillingly, for Frodo; Frodo and Sam do it, willingly, for each other and for the Shire; and Gandalf and Aragorn and their 7000 at the Black Gate do it for Frodo and Sam: "We must make ourselves the bait.... We must walk open-eyed into that trap."[27] As Christ did on the Cross. For He is not our exception but our rule.

The concrete particular way in which evil defeats itself is unforeseeable both by the good and by the evil. (Who foresaw 1989 in 1917?) Neither Sauron nor Gandalf anticipated the importance of Sam or Gollum, or just *how* "the pity of Bilbo may rule the fate of many" in sparing Gollum. It usually appears suddenly, as at the Crack of Doom, "the Dark Lord was suddenly aware of him [Frodo] . . . and the magnitude of his own folly was revealed to him in a blinding flash."[28] I think each of the damned will experience some such sudden "blinding flash" or Miserific Vision, like that face in Dore's illustration of Dante's "Inferno."

Yet, while we are surprised when we first come to the Crack of Doom in Volume III, we are not surprised. For in that consummation we recognize (re-cognize, remember) the truth; we recognize all the characters and many of the events of this story now. They are familiar to us because they are all parts of us. This is our story. It is a mirror. We are fascinated by it most deeply because of its truth. It is not even its beauties that pierce our hearts like swords (C. S. Lewis's words), or even its utter goodness that captivates us. (If books could be canonized as saints, this one would make it in a breeze.) No, it arrests us most powerfully because it is true. It is eternal truth made flesh. Only a great myth can do that astonishing feat, can translate the eternal truth of good and evil into the radically other medium of a temporal story. It makes the abstract concrete, the invisible visible, the Word flesh. (It is the opposite of pornography, which is the flesh made word. That is why there is no pornography in the great myth.)

Tolkien's mythopoec strategy is the exact counter to Satan's. It will take a minute to explain this.

Evil can work only in darkness. Even a vampire cannot stand the sun.

Good can work only in the light. Even the world's best surgeon cannot perform an operation if the hospital lights go out.

Every moral evil presupposes moral ignorance. Plato saw that; he only failed to trace it back one more step: the moral ignorance further presupposes an ignoring, which is an act of the will.

But our will is by its nature attracted to good, not evil, as our mind by its nature is attracted to truth, not falsehood. So Satan has to bend that attraction by sophistry and propaganda and advertising, the world's oldest profession. ("See this nice apple? You need this apple. Try it, you'll like it. You can afford it: the price is only one measly soul. What does it profit a man to lose the whole world and gain only his own soul?") By the way, the profession that is usually called the world's oldest depends on this older one for its success. All sin does. If sin didn't *seem* like fun, we'd all be saints. The origin of sin is advertising, the substitution of image for substance, appearance for reality. It's no accident that the New Testament calls Satan "the prince of the power of the air": ABC, NBC, CBS, MTV—he is the master of the media, where image is everything.

But he has to bait the hook of falsehood with the worm of truth, for no man will believe pure lies, as no fish will bite a naked hook. For instance, "If you eat that forbidden fruit, you will know evil as well as good." That was true. The lie was that they would be "like God," knowing good and evil in the same way God knows them. That's like saying a drunk knows sobriety and drunkenness in the same way a sober person does. The lie is the hook, the truth is the bait.

Well, to catch a thief, use a thief. If the devil baits the hook of falsehood with the worm of truth, the mythmaker and poet and storyteller baits the hook of truth with the worm of myth. Sometimes the worm is as short as one of Jesus' 50-word parables. Sometimes it is as long as Tolkien's 500,000-word epic, the Greatest Worm of the Century. And the fish defeats itself by taking the bait.

6. Evil Is Used for Good

Divine providence is like a French chef, using spices from decayed organisms to make good food even better. That all things, even evil, work together for good, is as familiar as Romans 8:28, but it never ceases to be startling that "God writes straight with crooked lines"; that even "sin is behovable," or good for something, as Lady Julian of Norwich says. The clearest case is the Crucifixion: the greatest evil in history, deicide, being used as the cause of the greatest good in history, salvation. And this is not a "case," not an example of some general principle; it is the real energizing center that gives all examples of it something of its own truth and power.

The Lord of the Rings is not theological, in that God never appears, as He does in *The Silmarillion*. Yet in a sense God is the main character. As the primary Author, He places into His story abundant clues to His existence, such as so-called coincidences, designs that can be seen in the threads on the backside of the tapestry. The image is from Thornton Wilder's *The Bridge of San Luis Rey*: life is a tapestry woven by God and therefore beautiful beyond telling, perfect beyond hope. But only in the next life can we see this perfect beauty. What we see here, on the back side of the tapestry, is loose ends of threads. Yet there are just enough clues, even in the mess of human life, and certainly in the order of nature, to make it reasonable to believe in and trust the wisdom and goodness of the Weaver. Even Woody Allen says, in "Love and Death," that "I'm an atheist, thank God; but on a good day I could believe in a Divine Mind pervading all parts of the known universe—except, of course, certain areas of northern New Jersey."

Here are just a few of the many providential "loose threads":

One is the *timing* of Frodo's first encounter with the Elves in the Shire: exactly at the moment when he was about to yield to the temptation to put on the Ring to hide from the Black Riders as one came sniffing for him.[29] We have all experienced such perfect timings in our lives; that is why we do not instinctively reject this as unrealistic.

Another is the need for apparently tragic events like Merry and Pippin being captured by the Orcs. Gandalf says that "they were brought to Fangorn and their coming was like the falling of small stones that starts an avalanche in the mountains."[30] "Is not that strange? Nothing that we have endured of late has seemed so grievous as the treason if Isengard... yet ... between them our enemies have contrived only to bring Merry and Pippin with marvelous speed, and in the nick of time, to Fangorn, where otherwise they would never have come at all."[31]

The clearest example, of course, is Gollum: sparing him, finding him, using him to sneak into Mordor, and of course his completing the whole Quest at the Crack of Doom. No one else could ever have done it!

Some of these providential uses of evil for good are tiny, like Barliman Butterbur's forgetfulness to deliver Gandalf's message. (Barliman, like myself and probably Tolkien, has A.D.D.—Attention Deficit Disorder.) As Aragorn tells him when he asks what he can possibly do against Mordor, "Not much, Barliman, but every little bit helps."[32] It does. Our salvation has sometimes hung on a thread. If a cheap Egyptian tailor had not cheated on the threads of Joseph's mantle, it would not have come apart in the hands of Potiphar's wife when Joseph fled from her seduction, and there would have been no physical evidence to convict Joseph and put him in prison at her accusation, and he would not have interpreted the dreams of his fellow prisoners, Pharaoh's ex-butler, who was to be returned to favor, and his ex-baker, who was to be killed, so that years later, when Pharaoh had the dream of the seven skinny cows eating the seven fat cows and could find no sage to interpret it, the butler could finally remember Joseph (he had A.D.D. too) and tell Pharaoh about him, with the result that Joseph interpreted the dream and convinced Pharaoh to store extra grain from the seven fat years to prevent starvation during the seven lean years, and only because of that was there grain in Egypt to escape starvation and survive, later to multiply to a million under Moses at the time of the Exodus. There would be no Jews, no Chosen People, and no Jesus if it were not for one weak thread in Joseph's mantle. We owe our salvation to a cheap Egyptian tailor. Divine providence has a sense of humor that is, as we say in Boston, "bizaah."

It may be a bizarre design, but it is not "a tale told by an idiot, full of sound and fury, signifying nothing." That is our culture's philosophy of life, in which "it" just happens. We need this story badly.

My last four points are about four of the strongest but most overlooked weapons against evil: sacrifice, humility, friendship, and words.

7. Sacrifice

The one power evil is utterly helpless before is sacrifice. In the book of Revelation, the lamb (*arnion*, "wee little lamb") defeats the beast (*therion*, monstrous and terrifying) by his blood, his death. Because it worked on Calvary, it works everywhere, since Calvary is the rule, not the exception.

Sacrifice is the height of love, the apogee of *agape*, and *agape* is the nature of God. And God has no rival. "Who is like God?" That is the meaning of the name "Michael," the archangel who is Gandalf to Satan's Sauron.

Frodo, Gandalf, and Aragorn are all, in different senses, martyrs, Christ-figures, who undergo different kinds of voluntary deaths and resurrections. Christ's tomb was a rock, Gandalf's was the abyss of Moria, Aragorn's was the Paths of the Dead, and Frodo's was the effect of the Ring on his spirit, a disease incurable in Middle-earth. The Elves, like Frodo, give up the whole world, since the power of the three eleven rings is now gone—although you may still see a few of them lingering on the west coast of Ireland if you have a sharp eye. Galadriel too saves Middle-earth by resisting the temptation: "'I pass the test,' she said. 'I will diminish and go into the West, and remain Galadriel.'"[33]

Frodo explains to Sam why he must go to the Grey Havens (death): "I have been too deeply hurt, Sam. I tried to save the Shire, and it has been saved, but not for me. It must often be so, Sam, when things are in danger: some one has to give them up, lose them, so that others may keep them."[34] The price is really paid, as on Calvary. "My life for yours" is the universal formula. It happens in every battle. Remember, Calvary is the rule, not the exception.

This is the very good news and very bad news. The good news is that it really works. Strength really is overcome by weakness, pride by humility, tyranny by martyrdom, Sauron by Frodo, Satan by Christ. The very bad news is that the price is real, and very steep. To slay evil's head, good's heel must bleed, and bleed forever in this world. "There are 1900 nails upon the Cross," wrote the poet in 1930.

This is not a principle for emergencies only. All of life is an emergency, in our world as well as in Tolkien's world. For there is no difference between our world and Tolkien's world. *The Lord of the Rings* is not set in some fantasy world but in our world. Middle-earth is the third rock from the sun. In this world, the self is saved only when it is lost, found only when really given away in sacrifice. True freedom comes only when you bind yourself to your duty.

The opposite of freedom is the power, which corrupts and enslaves. The Ring is a perfect symbol of this, for it is a closed circle, like a clenched fist, or a worm swallowing its own tail (the worm Oouroboros), and it encloses emptiness (the damned self). It is the exact opposite of the Cross.

As we know, but constantly forget, the Cross is the rule, not the exception. So is the Ring. What Gandalf tells Bilbo, Christ tells us: "It has got far too much hold on you. Let it go. And then you can go yourself and be free." And like Bilbo, we constantly reply, "I'll do as I choose and go as I please."[35]

To us too, as to Frodo on Amon Hen when he puts on the Ring and almost exposes himself to the Eye of Sauron, come inspirations from Gandalf to counter the one from Sauron: "Take it off! Take it off! Fool, take it off! Take off the Ring!"[36]

Eventually, it becomes impossible to take it off. Only Gollum can save Frodo at the Crack of Doom; only after Gollum has liberated Frodo from his finger and from the Ring, (as Beren was liberated from his hand and from the Silmaril by Carcharoth the great wolf of Angband in *The Silmarillion*) can it be said of Frodo that he "had been saved; he was himself again, he was free."[37]

Gollum is too far gone down that road to return: the road of losing the self by "finding" it, by grasping it. He cannot distinguish himself from the Ring; both are "the Precious." He rarely can even use the word "I" any more, the image of "I AM." His name is "we," or "Legion," for he is many. By grasping himself, and his power, and his freedom, and his Ring, he has lost himself, and his power, and his freedom, and his Ring. Down that road lives the Lieutenant of the Tower of Barad-dur, whom the captains of the Army of the West meet at the Black Gate: "his name is remembered in no tale; for he himself had forgotten it, and he said: 'I am the Mouth of Sauron.'"[38]

The reason why it is true in *The Lord of the Rings* that those who lose the self save it and those who save it lose it, is that Middle-earth is our earth; Tolkien's world is the real world. It is not just because Tolkien is a Christian but because a Christian is a realist.

8. Humility

Humility is a form of self-sacrifice: the sacrifice of pride and power. Only this willing "weakness" can defeat strength and force. Only Hobbits, not Men or Elves or Wizards, can get into Mordor; and only a Hobbit, at the Crack of Doom, can complete the task. Unless we become like little Hobbits, we cannot enter the Kingdom of Heaven. For the Lord became a little Hobbit, and He is the rule, not the exception, remember.

At the Council of Elrond the outcome of the principle of humility was foretold: "The road must be trod, but it will be very hard. And neither strength nor wisdom will carry us far upon it.... Such is oft the course of deeds that move the wheels of the world: small hands do them because they must, while the eyes of the great are elsewhere."[39]

9. Friendship

Like humility, friendship is a formidable weapon against evil. We are surprised to hear this. We cannot imagine a military propagandist, wondering how to frighten the troops of the enemy, coming up with this terrifying threat: "Our soldiers are loyal friends!" Yet friendship is strength, even in a military sense, because it unites, while weakness divides. "Divide and conquer" is the most elementary and practical military strategy. Friendship refuses to be divided, and thus refuses to be conquered. Any soldier knows that few men will do heroic deeds for abstract causes, even justice; but many will for their buddies, their friends.

The single force most responsible for winning the War of the Ring is Sam's friendship and love of Frodo. (Friendship is a form of love in pre-modern language.) The very title of Volume I, *The Fellowship of the Ring,* shows the centrality of friendship, or fellowship. It also shows that it is evil (the Ring) that elicits the strongest flowering of this great good in Middle-earth. Because our stories take place in the same place, the differences of time cannot change this truth. In our time too, for instance, the Irish and the English, who for many generations had been enemies killing each other, became friends who died for each other in the trenches of two great wars when Germany forged a Ring. What Germany did to the British, terrorists did to Americans.

Merry and Pippin (and of course Sam) are necessary to the success of the Quest, and only friendship brings them along. When Frodo tries to leave the Shire alone, so as not to endanger his friends, they form a conspiracy not to let him go alone. Frodo complains, "It does not seem that I can trust anyone," and Merry replies, "You cannot trust us to let you face trouble alone.... We are your friends, Frodo."[40]

There are doors that only friendship can open. For instance, the great Gate of Moria, which will respond to no force or spell of Gandalf's, but only to the word "friend" (*mellon*). The inscription said, "Speak, friend, and enter"; and Gandalf puzzled over what spell or password to speak, until he realized (as Saruman would never have done) that only the simple and innocent could solve this puzzle: "The translation should have been, 'Say (the word) "friend" and enter.' I had only to speak the Elvish word for *friend* and the doors opened.... Too simple for the learned loremaster in these suspicious days."[41] Or as we say in academia, only a Deconstructionist could miss it.

The culmination of Sam's friendship with Frodo is his carrying him up Mount Doom, like Christ carrying the Cross, or rather like Simon of Cyrene helping Christ carry His Cross to the end, as Frodo carries the Ring to the end. "To his amazement, he felt the burden light."[42] "He ain't heavy, he's my brother." We shouldn't be amazed; we were promised that: "My yoke is easy and My burden is light." The words of the old marriage ceremony make the same promise (marriages being, of course, the completest possible friendship): "Married life requires great sacrifice; only love can make it possible, and only perfect love can make it a joy."

10. Words

"In the beginning was the Word." That is why words have power over things. For it was in words that things were created. God first spoke the word, then the thing came to be, not vice versa. With us it is vice versa: we invent words to label pre-existing things, except when we "subcreate."

The Lord of the Rings shows this priority of words more clearly than any other book I know, because Tolkien tells us it began with his inventing a language, Elvish. Then there had to be Elves to speak it, and a world for them to live in, and events and stories in that world, and other species too: Wizards, Ents, Trolls, Orcs, Dwarves, Woses, Nazgúl, Hobbits, and even Men. (The fact that Tolkien insists on giving them capital letters is significant, as is the fact that we do not. In fact, the current fashion, unconsciously obeying our culture's increasing depersonalization, is to insist on lower-casing everything we possibly can. God created in capitals, and therefore so did Tolkien.)

In Tolkien's story, words have a power we usually call "magical," misunderstanding that word as a kind of short cut technology (as Tolkien explains in "On Fairy-Stories"). But it is very different: it is the "magic" of formal and final causality, not material and efficient causality (to use Aristotelian terminology). The inherent form (meaning) and purpose of a word flows over into material and visible effects, sacramentally, so that the word can effect what it signifies. Thus Bombadil's spell saves Merry from Old Man Willow and Frodo from the Barrow-wight: "None has ever caught him yet, for Tom, he is the master; His songs are stronger songs, and his feet are faster."[43] We are surprised to hear that song are "strong" only because we forget what we learned from *The Silmarillion:* that it was in music that God created the universe.

Frodo too has this "magical" power: when he calls Tom's name, two miracles happen, one spiritual and one physical: first, "with that name his voice seemed to grow strong," and second, Tom actually comes. If we find this unconvincing "magical," that reveals a lot about our religious life, and how much we have taken God at His word when he repeatedly promises the same thing Tom Bombadil does: "You just call out My name, and you know wherever I am, I'll come running to see you again. Winter, spring, summer or fall, all you've got to do is call, and I'll be there, yeah, yeah, yeah. You've got a Friend."

We all know there are magic words, words that sacramentally effect what they signify, like "I baptize thee" or "This is My Body." Two of the most familiar are "I love you" and "I hate you." These are not labels, these are weapons; arrows pierced through flesh into hearts. The whole of *The Lord of the Rings* is a great armor-piercing rocket; it can even get into our underground bunkers, our darkest inner Afghanistans.

The most powerful names are proper names, names of persons or places. When the Black Rider bangs on Fatty Bolger's door in Buckland saying "Open in the name of Mordor!" all the terror and power of Mordor are really present there. When Frodo, on Weathertop, faces the Black Rider, "he heard himself crying aloud, 'O Elbereth! Gilthoniel!'"[44] as he struck the Rider with his sword. Afterwards, Aragorn says, "All blades perish that pierce that dreadful King. More deadly to him was the name of Elbereth."[45]

In Shelob's lair Frodo again speaks in tongues: "Aiya Earendil Elenion Ancalima! He cried, and knew not what he had spoken; for it seemed that another voice spoke through his."[46] And then the tiny Hobbit with the tiny sword advanced on the most hideous living thing in Middle-earth with the phial of Galadriel and the name of Galadriel. A little later, Sam did the same: "'Galadriel!' he said faintly, and then he heard voices far off but clear: the crying of Elves as they walked under the stars in the beloved shadows of the Shire, and the music of the Elves... Gilthoniel A Elbereth! And then his tongue was loosed and his voice cried in a language which he did not know: 'A Elbereth Gilthoniel!'"[47]

"What's in a name?" "In the name of Jesus" devils are exorcised and the gate of Heaven is opened for us. What's in a name? Everything. In a name, the universe was created. That name was Christ, the Logos, the Mind of God, the creative Word of God. That is the sun whose beams we use when we subcreate: the Son of God.

"What's in a name?" Moses asked God that question at the burning bush, and God answered: "I am."

In a world where good is so fragile that a little evil can turn a whole world upside down, we wonder what is stronger. And we get the same answer.

Endnotes

1 J. R. R. Tolkien, *The Fellowship of the Ring* (New York: Ballantine Books, 1965), ix.
2 Ibid., pp. 24–25.
3 J. R. R. Tolkien, *The Return of the King* (New York: Ballantine Books, 1965), p. 179.
4 *Fellowship of the Ring*, p. 229.
5 Ibid., p. 225.
6 J. R. R. Tolkien, *The Two Towers* (New York: Ballantine Books, 1965), p. 204.
7 *Return of the King*, p. 367.
8 Ibid., p. 371.
9 *Two Towers*, p. 132.
10 *Return of the King*, p. 189.
11 Ibid., p. 197.
12 Ibid.
13 *Fellowship of the Ring*, p. 351.
14 *Two Towers*, p. 113.
15 *Return of the King*, p. 233.
16 Ibid., p. 244.
17 John 7:17.
18 *Two Towers*, pp. 49–50.
19 Ibid., p. 77.
20 *Fellowship of the Ring*, p. 354.
21 *Fellowship of the Ring*, p. 347.
22 II Corinthians 10:5.
23 Isaiah 7:9.
24 *Fellowship of the Ring*, p. 59.
25 Ibid., p. 94.
26 Ibid., p. 350.
27 *Return of the King*, p. 191.
28 Ibid., p. 275.
29 *Fellowship of the Ring*, p. 116.
30 *Two Towers*, p. 127.
31 Ibid., p. 126.
32 *Fellowship of the Ring*, p. 229.

33 Ibid., p. 474.
34 *Return of the King*, p. 382.
35 *Fellowship of the Ring*, p. 60.
36 *Two Towers*, p. 519.
37 *Return of the King*, p. 277.
38 Ibid., p. 202.
39 *Fellowship of the Ring*, p. 353.
40 Ibid., p. 150.
41 Ibid., p. 402.
42 *Return of the King*, p. 268.
43 *Fellowship of the Ring*, p. 196
44 Ibid., p. 263.
45 Ibid., p. 165.
46 *Two Towers*, p. 418.
47 Ibid., p. 430.

3

The Literary Backgrounds of *The Lord of the Rings*

Janet Leslie Blumberg

The origins of *The Lord of the Rings* in Tolkien's imagination go back to influences as diverse as the epics of Homer, the Judeo-Christian Scriptures, and the ancient Norse sagas—for Tolkien, like C. S. Lewis, was greatly drawn to that tragic atmospheric quality they called "pure Northernness." Still, I believe that the most important backgrounds for appreciating the literary artistry of Middle-earth are Anglo-Saxon poetry, written in Old English (A.D. 600-1000), and High Medieval English literature, written in Middle English, mostly in the time of Chaucer (fourteenth century). Further, I believe that the distinctive *uses* Tolkien made of these two literary legacies—and in one case his unusual blending of them—deserve to be called "pre-eminently high and beautiful."[1] When we consider these two bodies of writing—each medieval and each Christian, yet notably distinct from one another—we find ourselves being carried into the intimate workings of the mind of Tolkien, as a gifted creator of mythological worlds and narratives.

The Influence of Anglo-Saxon Poetry on Tolkien

The earlier of the two bodies of medieval English literature that so deeply influenced Tolkien comes to us from the period A.D. 600–1066, after the Fall of Rome left Roman-Celtic Britain vulnerable to the West Germanic invaders in the fifth century

A.D. It is difficult to grasp the peculiar intensity of Anglo-Saxon literature unless you have read it in its original Old English. The language, like the worldview, was spare and stark: a small store of basic root words was made to serve, rather than admitting new words from other languages. Instead of accepting and incorporating borrowed words, Anglo-Saxon extended its vocabulary by making evocative combinations of the monosyllabic roots already in its own "word-hoard," thus forming remarkable new compounds (*mildheortnes* for "grace") and figures of speech called *kennings*, such as "whale-path" to indicate the sea, or "word-hoard" to indicate a poet's linguistic resources. The language and the culture alike seem to reflect the harshness of life in the far North; for example, while the Celtic languages abound with words designating colors such as green and gold and crimson, Anglo-Saxon has very few "color" words. What color words do occur in Old English usually refer to the lightness or the darkness of things, whether something gleams, or is dusky or dull. *Wann under welkum* ("wan under the skies") is a conventional alliterative phrase in old Saxon battle poetry.

Equally in its themes and subjects, Old English literature is densely compressed and limited, concentrating on a narrow range of topics, but handled with incredible power and depth of feeling. The most beloved genres of the Anglo-Saxons were *riddles*, *hero tales* or *epic lays*, and *elegies*—exquisite songs of lament for the precious things that have passed away. The life experienced by these sea-going, war-faring peoples (whose later cousins would be, of course, the Vikings, who attempted their own invasion of England during the latter part of the Anglo-Saxon period) was generally limited to a harsh struggle against death and destruction, in which the one source of value and worth seems to have come from the bonds, celebrated everywhere in its literature, of love and loyalty between a battle-leader —*dryghten*—and the members of his retinue, his *thegns* or chief warrior followers. The Roman historian Tacitus described this Germanic social structure under the Latin term *comitatus*. A good translation might be "hearth-companions," or Tolkien's own translations in *The Lord of the Rings*: the "company" or the "fellowship." All activities seemed to arise out of and lead back into this central communal bond between *dryghten* and *thegn*. A woman fulfils her role as serving woman, wife, or princess, by filling cups around the hearth-fire in the mead hall during the long winter months, or perhaps by being given as a peace-pledge in betrothal to the son of the leader of another tribe. Relatively few articles of beauty or value existed—a golden cup, a jeweled sword—but what were possessed (often taken as plunder) were given as gifts to seal and commemorate the bonds between battle-lord and thegn. Because of the scarcity of words, of warmth, of hope, of alternatives, of precious objects, such as do occur are cherished and valued all the more. After one has read much of the extant poetry of Anglo-Saxon England, a parallelism emerges between everything that shines out, on the one hand, and the dark backdrop against which they shine, whether we mean the light of a campfire, or a bright helmet, or a peace-treaty through marriage, or the sacrificial courage of a warrior dying for his people, or the generosity of spirit (*mod*) shown by one's lord through the giving of gifts, or the songs of the bards, singing of these bright things, shining acts of heroism and the stories of creation.

Historically, the Anglo-Saxons overcame the Romanized Celts and settled down in their seven kingdoms in the main part of England (from "Angle-land"), pushing the Celts to the extremities of Wales and Scotland, and across the waters to Ireland and Brittany. (It was among these Celts that memories flourished of "Arthur," the native Roman-Celtic leader who tried in the fifth century to defend the Britons from the invading English. After the Norman Conquest, this Arthurian literature would re-enter England and be adopted as their own by the very peoples against whom the historical Arthur had fought.) The Saxons brought with them into England their tribal bards and their own rich store of poetry and legend. Presumably they worshipped a pantheon of Northern warrior gods similar to Thor and Odin; certainly they shared with their Finnish and Norse cousins the dark fatalism that (for the latter peoples, at least) took the form of the cosmic battle of Ragnarok at the end of time, in which the gods would fight on the right side, drawing to their cause all worthy human heroes, and yet all these gods and heroes would go down together in apocalyptic defeat to the monsters of Chaos and destruction. While we have no specific details about Anglo-Saxon pre-Christian religion, we can feel the ubiquity of the darkness and how it is lying in wait for all light and life, throughout the writings of the Anglo-Saxon period, and most particularly in the Anglo-Saxon elegies and in the famous poem *Beowulf*. But we have these works today because the Anglo-Saxons turned ardently to Christianity in the sixth and seventh centuries, and many Anglo-Saxons left their lives as battle-leaders and followers, as princesses or serving women in the mead halls and homesteads, and entered—both men and women—into the Benedictine monasteries that sprang up all over England. For the next three centuries, England was the beacon of stability and liberal learning in Europe, while most of the rest of Europe languished in the turmoil of the Dark Ages. In fact, during the reign of King Alfred (tenth century), the literacy rate in England was higher than it would be again *until the nineteenth century*. Alfred also had the *Bible* in Old English translation sent out to all the bishoprics in the land. And in the monasteries were written down and preserved many works of literary art (though we have only a fraction of what must have been produced), and these were composed in the old bardic manner, drawing upon the traditional pre-Christian strong-stress meters, by monastic writers highly skilled in the Old English alliterative line.

The period as a whole and all of its art and literature show a peculiar fusion of old and new. The author of *Beowulf*, for example, reflects "a moment of poise in a vast transitional movement." These are Tolkien's own descriptive words, in his brilliant 1936 critical essay titled "*Beowulf*: The Monsters and the Critics."[2] The "vast transitional movement" Tolkien has in mind is the one that will culminate in the thoroughly Christianized thought-world of the High Medieval world-picture that emerges in the twelfth through the fourteenth centuries, with the writings, for example, of Aquinas, Dante, Chaucer, and the *Pearl*-poet. (As we shall be discussing, Tolkien taught and published on the English literature of both of these medieval periods). In view of the splendid High Medieval cultural culmination that will burst forth in England in the fourteenth century (especially in the works of Chaucer and the *Pearl*-poet), Tolkien spends a great deal of time in his *Beowulf* essay describing the mind-set of the eighth-century *Beowulf*-poet, with whom Tolkien seems to identify deeply:

> ... it is the mood of the author, the essential cast of his imaginative apprehension of the world, that is my concern.... And in [his] poem I think we may observe... a fusion that has occurred *at a given point* of contact between old and new, a product of deep thought and emotion.... One of the most potent elements in that fusion is the Northern courage: the theory of courage, which is the great contribution of early Northern literature.... But in England this imagination was brought into touch with Christendom, and with the Scriptures. The process of 'conversion' is a long one, but some of its effects were doubtless immediate: an alchemy of change (producing ultimately the [high] medieval) was at once at work.... the minds which still retain [the traditions of the dark Northern world] are changed, and the memories viewed in a different perspective: *at once they become more ancient and remote, and in a sense* [even] *darker....*

Tolkien imagines here that the ancient pre-Christian legacy of the Northern "theory of courage" is being held in the deeply sorrowing mind of an Anglo-Saxon artist who has accepted the Christian hope, and who is comforted by it, but who yet chooses to tell a story of a pre-Christian king, a good king who chose to fight to preserve the good, in spite of an inevitable, certain defeat. Why so?

> A Christian was (and is) still like his forefathers a mortal hemmed in a hostile world. The monsters [the mythological adversaries of gods and men in the old religion] remained the enemies of mankind, the infantry of the old war, and became inevitably the enemies of the one God, *ece dryghten*, the eternal captain of the new. Even so the vision of the war changes. For it begins to dissolve, even as the contest on the fields of Time thus takes on its largest aspect. The tragedy of the great temporal defeat remains for a while poignant, but ceases to be finally important. It is no defeat, for the end of the world is part of the design of *Metod*, the Arbiter who is above the mortal world. Beyond there appears a possibility of eternal victory....

But the shift is not complete in *Beowulf*.... The author is still concerned primarily with man on earth, rehandling in a new perspective an ancient theme: that man, each man and all men, and all their works shall die. A theme no Christian need despise. Yet this theme plainly would not be so treated, but for the nearness of a pagan time. The shadow of its despair, if only as a mood, as an intense emotion of regret, is still there. The worth of the defeated valour of this world is deeply felt.

We gain a new appreciation for the tone and the mood of *The Lord of the Rings* when we read these thoughts of Tolkien the literary critic, defending the veiled sense of hope and the unveiled sense of loss and regret in the early, eighth-century Anglo-Saxon masterwork *Beowulf*. Like *The Lord of the Rings*, written by a devout Christian, *Beowulf* also (Tolkien believes) was written by a devout Christian, in whose mind "new scripture and old tradition touched and ignited." Like *The Lord of the Rings*, which Tolkien would begin writing within a year after this essay, *Beowulf* is:

a poem dealing of design with the noble pagan of old days.... Man alien in a hostile world, engaged in a struggle which he cannot win while the world lasts, is assured that his foes are the foes also of *Dryghten*, that his courage noble in itself is also the highest loyalty: so said *thyle* and clerk. In *Beowulf* we have, then.... a poem by a learned man writing of old times, who looking back on the heroism and sorrow feels in them something permanent and something symbolical....His poem is a greater contribution to early medieval thought than the harsh and intolerant view that consigned the heroes to the devil.

"... a learned man writing of old times." Tolkien meditates at length in the 1936 *Beowulf* essay on such a figure, whom he defends against the aspersions of modern literary critics. A few months later, as he began writing his "new Hobbit," a book that turned into an epic-length narrative about the heroes of the Third Age, Frodo and Sam, Gandalf and Strider, Tolkien had this portrait of a fellow-artist ready-made to guide him:

As the poet looks back into the past, surveying the history of kings and warriors in the old tradition, he sees that all glory (or as we might say 'culture' or 'civilization') ends in night.... We get in fact a poem from a pregnant moment of poise, looking back into the pit, by a man learned in old tales who was struggling, as it were, to get a general view of them all, perceiving their common tragedy of inevitable ruin, and yet feeling this the more poetically because he himself was removed from the direct pressure of its despair. He could view from without, but still feel immediately from within, the old dogma: despair of the event [the outcome], combined with faith in the value of doomed resistance. He was still dealing with the great temporal tragedy, and not yet writing an allegorical homily in verse.

Here Tolkien concisely indicates where medieval Christian literature is headed—"allegorical homily in verse," such as we find in the later *Piers Plowman* or *The Divine Comedy* or in parts of *The Canterbury Tales*—without denigrating an incipient Anglo-Saxon Christianity that is still in close touch with the fatalistic and mythological qualities of Northern heroic verse. For Tolkien, *Beowulf* is mythic rather than allegorical; although written by a Christian, it suppresses both the old pagan religion and the new Christian devotion, in order to focus on the common theme of doomed mortality and courageous loyalty. What is so fascinating about the influence on Tolkien from this poem and this period is that he is drawn powerfully to *Beowulf* and other Anglo-Saxon works, *precisely* by the fact that in them the ascendancy of the new Christian order *is not yet complete*. I mean to say that it is the darkness, the spareness, the fatalism even, of Old English literature that he cherishes most particularly, and that he shows he cherishes specifically in a work he believed was written by a Christian. Why had such a poem so great an appeal for Tolkien that he came to set his own long hero-tale in a similarly "heroic-elegaic" setting and at its own "moment of poise" in a vast historical transition from the Third Age of Middle-earth to the Fourth, at a time when all things are being weighed in the balance? (Frodo's quest "stands upon the edge of a knife." And in it, so does the history of Middle-earth.)

To move toward a fuller answer to this question, let me discuss four exceedingly characteristic high points in Anglo-Saxon literature: the elegies, *Beowulf*, "The Battle of Malden," and the parable of the sparrow from Bede's church history of the English people.

The elegy is a powerful ancient genre that produced exquisite lyrical songs of loss and lament in all of the European literatures; we see it as an important form among the ancient Greeks.
In Latin literature, the elegy was sometimes signaled by a series
of lines beginning with *ubi sunt*, "Where are they now...." In
our own times, we have heard the pure elegiac mode in the
nineteen-sixties folk song that asks, "Where have all the flowers
gone?" and adds the haunting refrain, "long time passing...."
What always matters particularly about elegy is its *blending of
love and sorrow*: but the grieving speaker in an Anglo-Saxon elegiac poem is participating in the central theme of the entire
Anglo-Saxon culture, when engaging in this melancholy look-
ing-backwards over the years in order to keep faith with and
practice the deepest loyalty to precisely those good things and
good persons who inevitably, by their very nature, will pass
away and be lost. (Thus Strider cherishes the memory of Arwen
and the goodness that will make her mortal, along with all
things Elvish, fated to be sundered from Middle-earth, and the
nobility of the kings of old who have passed away under the
shadow of Mordor. This is a love and loyalty against all odds
and in despite of any earthly certainty of the fulfilment of
desire.)

In other words, in the Anglo-Saxon elegiac, the conventional
elegiac speaker feels an immediate loss or separation in the context of a larger "historical" setting contrived by the poet; always
such an elegiac speaker presupposes a long and dark historical
background that lends depth and poignancy to the current
lament. It takes a poet, like Tolkien, to recognize this for what it
is in artistic terms: an "illusion" employed by the author to
poetic ends. In 1936 Tolkien told the community of medievalists
that the historical allusions in Beowulf were just that: not historical facts but poetic allusions, figures of speech employed to
heighten the mythic significance of Beowulf's death by setting it
in an elegiac context, that is, one that gives "the illusion of historical perspective." Tolkien had no particular quarrel with the
historian's interest in those allusions as clues to the actual history of the Geats, just as he had no quarrel with readers who
might wish to delve more deeply into the earlier ages of Middle-earth by reading the materials in *The Silmarillion* for their
own sake. But in either case we have an author who nonethe-

less, in the crafting of the immediate literary work, is employing such backgrounds not as themselves the center of interest, but for a specific, purely artistic purpose: to create for the heroes of the narrative the kind of depth and sadness—the sense of "a past already dark and weighted with regret"—that constitutes the Anglo-Saxon elegiac setting. (Interestingly, Peter Jackson's beautiful film of *The Fellowship of the Ring* replaces the Aragorn of Tolkien's imagination, who is a wise and battle-hardened Anglo-Saxon elegiac speaker, with the more familiar and conventional—in *our* times—figure of the sensitive and self-doubting Romantic lover as played by Viggo Mortensen in the movie.)

Several poignant Anglo-Saxon elegies have come down to us: among them "The Wanderer," "The Seafarer," and "The Wife's Lament." In these sorrowing lamentations we always listen to a conventionally weary "elegiac speaker"—typically an exile whose former *dryghten* and hearth-companions have been killed in battle (although a woman who mourns her cruel separation from her husband through treachery may also serve). In Anglo-Saxon elegy, the imagery is stunningly bleak and lonely: the old warrior of "The Wanderer" leaves behind all comfortable human habitations and "stirs" *mid hondum* ("with hands") *hrim-cealde sae* ("the icy-cold sea"). Something is calling to these speakers, re-awakening their yearnings, compelling them to seek far away in time or in space the memory of the beloved person or the times of fellowship they now carry within themselves only as vivid and burning memories. Yet these elegiac speakers remain utterly devoted; the worth of what is remembered and mourned is heightened, not weakened, by their loss and absence.

Such was the devotion of the Anglo-Saxons to the elegiac mood that, as Tolkien rightly pointed out in 1936, *Beowulf* itself is not a typical "epic" at all: it is instead an extended elegy, or better, an "heroic-elegaic" poem. In all its 3000-plus lines, Tolkien states, the poem is "a prelude to a dirge, perhaps the most moving ever written."

Nothing, however, is more heroic-elegaic than the two famous lines in "The Battle of Malden," an Anglo-Saxon battle poem written in the tenth century right after a terrible English loss to the Vikings, because of which the Vikings overran a large area of East Anglia. The children, the women, the fields, the animals were plundered and taken. Even though such a terrible price was paid because of this disastrous defeat, the poem nonetheless concentrates in the Northern style upon the loyalty of the battle-leader's retainers, as they fight to the death around their slain lord. One by one, in their final speeches, they make their battle-boasts, speeches that allow the courage and loyalty within their hearts (inside the *hord-cofa*, "treasure-chest or coffer") to shine out brilliantly in the midst of the carnage, where the carrion-eaters will soon be wheeling overhead (another convention of old Saxon battle poetry).

This tragic scene is strangely heightened not only because it is, after all, the scene of a horrendous defeat, but also because the poet has already described in detail exactly how the defeat had come about: it was through the *dryghten*'s own "noble" error or misjudgment. His was an act of goodness and generosity, or at least of honor, that had voluntarily given up the tactical advantage to the enemy (the poet calls this *ofermod*, or an excess of *mod*, the same Anglo-saxon term that is used elsewhere to describe the origin of Satan's rebellion against God). Yet these loyal *thegns* do not waver or rebuke the memory of their lord, as they exhort one another to stand fast by his body and to die with him. What the poem celebrates in this highly ironic and bitter setting is that shining inwardness that may gleam out even, or especially, at the very moment of death. It is in this scene, accordingly, that one of the *dryghten*'s followers rallies the others with these remarkable and famous words of gnomic wisdom:

Hige sceal the heardra, heorte the cenre,

Mod sceal the mare, the ure maegen lytlath.

"High (spirit) shall be harder, heart (shall be) the keener, (our) *mod* shall be the more, even as our might (our may-en) littleth"—that is, grows littler, diminishes, and fades away to nothing. The inward truth, residing in the treasure chest or *breast-cofa* of goodness within the *dryghten* and within his followers—these shall be even more manifest, when each unflinching hero is being overwhelmed and destroyed by the enemy.

This certainly gives us a clue as to how the death of God on the Cross will be understood by the Anglo-Saxon peoples. The stoical warrior ethic seen in "The Battle of Malden" is of course what Tolkien calls in his *Beowulf* essay, "the Northern theory of courage." In this theory, "defeat is thought no refutation." (Remember that in Norse cosmology, even the gods and heroes were doomed finally to go down into nothingness, along with every kind of life ever nurtured by the World-tree in its temporal ages....) In the face of such an inevitable fatality, all that matters is what is held within the heart, within the warrior's chest, locked away and brooded over and kept faith with: the bonds of remembrance that undergird loyalty and trust, that still flame out, even in the midst of storm and darkness, in just the way that once, around the campsite as the company shares bread together, a hero of old named Sam began to sing: "Gil-galad was an Elven king. / Of him the harpers sadly sing...." (The recent film drops out almost all of the poetry, legend, and communal artistry that abounds and plays such a significant role in Tolkien's imaginative universe, and so, despite excellent casting and the great personal appeal of the actors, we lose that sense of deeper inwardness we feel in Tolkien's own Sam, Frodo, Gandalf, or Aragorn, an inwardness that is based on their histories of attention to the songs and narratives of the past. One might be caused to wonder: do modern "persons" in general possess *horde-cofas*? What treasures do we store up, and with what do we inwardly keep faith? Do we seek or even register the deeper inwardness that comes from absorbing and meditating upon a rich legacy of text?)

What is valued in an Anglo-Saxon poem does not depend on success for its value. Nor does its worth ever shine more brightly than in the gift-giving of sacrificial death by a warrior willing to die for others. (Compare Tolkien's treatment of the horn of Boromir and his redemptive death....) This is the stoical Northern vision of life: darkness countered only by personal commitment to a few bright and infinitely precious bonds that give to life its only larger or deeper significance. And this is also the spirit in which many Anglo-Saxons originally understood Christianity.

In early Anglo-Saxon representations of Christ and the Good News, the heroic-elegaic context is compelling. One native poet of the sixth century, in "The Dream of the Rood" (that is, "The Dream of the Cross"), took the dark Northern heroic worldview and made it a stunningly effective context for the Gospel. Further, the poet does this by combining all three of the primary Anglo-Saxon genres: the riddle, the hero-tale, and the elegy. The poem opens with a conventional elegiac speaker—weary and lonely after the loss of his lord, unable to rest while all others are sleeping. To him appears a mysterious riddle-tree blazing with light: the tree confronts the speaker and tells its personal story of being uprooted, *ic waes aheawen* ("I was hewn down") *holtes on ende* ("turned on end") and made into a gallows for criminals. By the time we and the speaker realize the riddlespeaker is a tree-turned-gallows, the riddles have come to grow considerably more baffling, as the tree tells how it saw coming toward it *the yeong haeleth* ("the young hero"), and recounts its steadfast loyalty to this courageous *dryghten*, the battle leader who ascends upon the tree "in the presence of many enemies."

The tree makes its battle-boast: it would have liked to have fought for its *dryghten* by felling all his enemies with a mighty swoop, but "that was not the will of my lord." So, exactly like the young hero, the tree, too, stands firm. Thus the tree chooses to be cut down in death with its master. The riddle-tree cannot resist making a withering remark at this point, about the lord's *other* followers, the disciples: "they were cowardly and ran away…." Then the tree is thrown down and discarded, but the risen Master's followers find it and it is lifted on high and decked with jewels and gold. The poem concludes with a marvelous evocation of salvation not by works but by faith, in which all who bear *on breostum* ("on/in their breast") the sign of this riddle-tree will not fear to stand before the Master at the end of days. (The descriptive phrase signifies both the physical cross worn on a chain and the inward, spiritual faithfulness of the warrior-tree's character, based on its total identification with Christ in His death and rebirth. These two meanings—physical and spiritual—are not separate, but indissolubly one, in keeping with the spontaneously mythic way of thinking found in most traditional or pre-modern societies.)

At the end of "The Dream of the Rood," the original elegiac speaker (to whom the dream-vision appears) remains an exile and a wanderer, still very much the conventional elegiac wisdom-figure of Anglo-Saxon elegy. But he has responded to the Tree's witness, and he has joined a new company of hearth-companions, those who follow and are willing to die for a *dryghten* who chooses death and opens a way to life for his people. The world of this inspired apologetical poem remains very dark indeed, yet the integrity and valor of the young hero, and the offered place of loving and being loved by him as a member of his loyal retinue, redeems (although it does not dispel) the dark elegiac of life on this earth. The speaker looks forward to a far-off reunion, somewhere and sometime, beyond this life. By joining the *comitatus* of mortal sufferers, the Christian *Dryghten* has given a surety that what the speaker knows and loves as good, will not perish forever. ("'Here is the heart of Elvendom on earth,' Aragorn said, 'and here my heart dwells ever, unless there be a light beyond the dark roads that we must still tread, you and I. Come with me!' And taking Frodo's hand in his, he left the hill of Cerin Amroth and came there again never as living man.")

For all Anglo-Saxon poetic speakers, *Lif is laene: eal scaeceth leoht and lif somod* ("Life is transitory: light and life together hasten away"). A light starts – *lixte se leoma ofer landa fela* ("its radiance gleamed over many lands")—and there is the sound of music, but the outer darkness and its hostile offspring "lie ever in wait for the torches to fail and the voices to cease." A light starts and spreads over many lands—and then goes out. Tolkien used this imagery of small points of light against a vast encompassing darkness whenever he wrote about the old Northern theory of courage, and this is the same imagery used everywhere in Anglo-Saxon literature itself. Even the Old English church historian Bede, chronicling the conversion of his people to Christianity, uses this kind of image when he records the famous Anglo-Saxon parable in which a man's life is described as being "like a swallow." The swallow flies into the mead hall from out of the darkness of storm and wind, and for a brief time it enjoys the warmth and fellowship and hears the music and laughter, as *dryghten* and *thegns* feast together and listen to the harpers around the fire during the long winter months. But then, all to soon, the bird flies out again at the other end of the mead hall, flies back out into the storm and darkness of which it knows nothing. After offering this parable, the chief counselor of the king of Northumbria urges the king to welcome the new Christian faith, if it offers any greater knowledge of the meaning of human life, and any larger context within which to live and act.

When you think of the legacy of what Tolkien absorbed from Anglo-Saxon literature, then think of a dark and fatalistic worldview that does not fear darkness or run away from the battle. Even in defeat, what matters is *mod*—the inward goodness that gleams out more strongly ("mod shall be the more") when we are being overwhelmed and defeated. All human beings know about "the great temporal defeat," but not all know or trust in a faithfulness that transcends death. In this Old English setting, what God suffers on the Cross reveals God's generosity and goodness, God's truly faithful inwardness, in a manner in which no other event or action could do. One is reminded of Augustine's exclamation: "*O felix culpa*—Oh fortunate fall (of man), that has occasioned so great a Redeemer." The generous, large-hearted, infinitely loving *mod* of God that was hidden in Christ shone out on the cross for all to see, precisely when His strength most "diminished" and was overwhelmed by the burden of temporal sin and evil, and by the burden of simple mortality. While it is the case that virtually any just battle at any time in history might provide a "temporary stay against confusion," only in the Fourth Age of Middle-earth, the coming Age of Men, will the hidden Providence of Middle-earth Itself carry the battle to the enemy by striking at the very core of the problem, the presence of inward evil inside every human heart. By the action of the Cross, through an ultimate sacrificial death, God will break the power of evil within the heart, and will initiate a new inner life in that place. Then there will be a warfare that is fully spiritual and psychological and personalistic. But in the previous ages, the conflict of darkness and light can be treated mythically and poetically, as though they are external forces struggling for worldly control. We cannot read Tolkien well by measuring *The Lord of the Rings* against the canons of realism and psychological complexity proper to the novel, a new genre befitting the new age of modernity. We must read Tolkien as an epic poet and as an heroic-elegaic mythological maker, or we will risk missing his real accomplishments.

So, when you think of Tolkien's debt to Anglo-Saxon literature and its worldview, think of its darkness and its undefeated loyalties. Think of the elegiac mood, and the beloved wisdom-figure of the elegiac speaker. And think also of the sea and the Anglo-Saxon yearning for the sea, the yearning for something transcendent and beyond what is known and familiar. Yet think too of the deep-rootedness and earthiness of this literature and its sense of the living personalities within trees and caves and spiders—or within swords, for that matter—all named and celebrated in Middle-earth, as they were among the Old English songs of the bards.

The presence of the Anglo-Saxon poetic makes itself felt forcefully throughout Middle-earth. There is the love of riddles, shared by Hobbits with the closely related people from whom Smeagol is derived. The entrance to Khazad-dhum states an Elvish riddle that stumps even Gandalf the Grey. The continuous birthday-present-giving of the Shire's inhabitants is a trivialization of the nearly forgotten tribal custom of gift-giving, the custom that cemented the all-important bonds between battle leader and *thegn*. The animistic voices of trees and other natural kinds—the fish, the whale, and so forth—who speak in Anglo-Saxon riddles, reflect a fully personalized tribal world. (Does the depersonalized world of large technological societies impose a special burden upon the often isolated and alienated members of the modern 'masses'?). There seems to have been a special significance of the Tree in Anglo-Saxon and perhaps older Druidic times, which remains with us in the yule log or in the forests that march to seal Macbeth's doom. (Tolkien's intense anti-modernism may have begun with the felling of a beautiful tree he loved in childhood. The tree was left lying where it fell and the child was bewildered by the insistent arbitrary malice of the industrialized society he saw around him.) The four Hobbits who return from the quest to find Sharkey in control of the Shire are able to "raise the Shire" because the old tribal customs are not entirely forgotten among the now-settled Halflings. Likewise, the ranger-duties undertaken by the men of Dunedain, who range Middle-earth to protect and preserve it, remind us of the wise and battle-hardened exiles who speak in the Anglo-Saxon elegies, brooding over the ways of mortal men with deep nostalgia and regret. In Anglo-Saxon literature we find the horn and its winding, we find the bright swords that carry like seasoned warriors their own genealogies or battle histories, and we find the various monsters and night-walkers that stand in mythically for all of the threatening darknesses with which a war-faring people is threatened. Even the name of Middle-earth comes from the Anglo-Saxon compound word for the habitable world, *middengeard*, and most of the poetry of Middle-earth is written in one or another variation upon the old Germanic strong-stress meter, with alliteration used (rather than rhyming) for construction of the verse-line.[3]

But the most fascinating of all of Tolkien's uses of Anglo-Saxon poetry is the deeper one I have been laboring to bring into view. It is Tolkien's decision to locate his own epic narrative within an heroic-elegaic moment in the history of Middle-earth. For his own artistic purposes, he created an "illusion of historical depth" by setting his new story against the backdrop of the first three Ages of Middle-earth, full of its own hero tales and shimmering with a mythic cosmology in which the heart is torn between "the worth of the defeated valour of this world" and the veiled gleams of a consolation to come from beyond "the great temporal tragedy." It is especially remarkable that Tolkien chose the Anglo-Saxon heroic-elegaic mood and its melancholy outlook for *The Lord of the Rings*, because Tolkien could have chosen to adapt the other, later, High Medieval and overtly Christian cosmic vision for his work (as Tolkien felt that C. S. Lewis tended to do): the triumphantly Christian vision that we find vitally alive in medieval European masterpieces such as Dante's *Divine Comedy*, the *Summa* of Thomas Aquinas, and Chaucer's *Canterbury Tales*.

If the old Northern fatalism amounted to a worldview in which darkness was ontologically supreme (pre-eminently strong and enduring), then in those literatures we have a cosmos so beset by darkness and evil—by the "monsters of Chaos and unreason," in Tolkien's words—that against them only a few brief flickers of goodness are able to spring up, where loyal men support their *dryghten* and die for the people, even though none can long survive. Ontologically (that is, in terms of its "being"), this is a world that is darker even than the worldviews offered us in most of the dualisms with which we are familiar. Platonism, for example, or Gnosticism envision two universal forces at work in the cosmos, good and evil, light and darkness, spirit and body—locked into a universal metaphysical struggle against one another. This is dark enough, but even darker is the Nordic worldview, in which even divinity itself cannot hold off forever the ultimate victory of the dark. The gods themselves, finally, will die, fighting the good fight along with all worthy human warriors. In contrast, therefore, to ontological dualism (good and evil as roughly equal and opposite entities), I would like to call the Northern cosmology fatalistic, in the sense that it leans toward a kind of monism of darkness. Light and life are too brief and flickering to offer any serious resistance; there is no effective ontological counterbalance to evil. Yet within this outlook, the human heart still remembers and pays tribute to "the defeated valour" of this world.

What is so important for us to consider is that Tolkien well knew that Christianity brought to the early English converts a worldview that is neither fatalistic nor dualistic. The scriptural tradition in general, and Western European Christianity in particular, reveal ontological dualism to be deeply problematic, because of the biblical insistence upon a divinely good creation of the universe by an ultimate Being who is entirely good. This monism of original goodness was explicitly worked out in the thought of Augustine of Hippo and was well-known in Benedictine Christianity (even though in both cases dualism creeps back in when considering how to live the Christian life). Although the struggle of light against darkness may for the Christian often *appear* dualistic, or even fatalistic, from a merely earthly perspective, nonetheless the incarnational vision of the Christian affirmation sees every temporal thing as innately good in its nature, originating in its being from God, and still held in being by the divine Being in spite of sin. The striking Augustinian theory of evil, then, makes evil only a temporal (but not finally victorious) twisting or bending of the good. Ultimately, evil does not "exist," because it is merely the negative measure of "the degree of ruin" into which the original thing has fallen. (Evil is the name of the *difference* between the perfect fulfillment of the intrinsic nature of any thing, and the dysfunction of that nature brought about by the woundedness called sin.)

Yet because Christians believe that humanity and the entire earth have fallen into darkness, there is a sense in which the fatalism of the Northern mythic imagination makes sense to the early Christian heart. In history, death and loss are ubiquitous. One can resonate with and endorse the Nordic sense of doom within the sphere of human history, while still knowing that beyond it and circumscribing its darkness, the eternal light of the encircling heavens shines (so Sam is comforted by looking at the stars, on the very last leg of his journey with Frodo), and a Source of life abides that cannot be destroyed. Therefore, for the Christian mind, those small and flickering campfires are no longer alone; they are unknowingly "keeping faith," as it were, with that transcendent reality of a heavenly light beyond all earthly darkness. Such a Christian perspective cannot help but praise the campfires that blazed and then went out, long before hope of an otherworldly rescue ever came into sight. The faithfulness of the pre-Christian heart is if anything more remarkable, more pure, than the faithfulness that *knows* it will be rewarded (so Lewis reminds us of the danger that always resides in Christianity of a distortion of the Good News into "theological hedonism"). Only those faithful choosings that would side with the good even in its utter defeat can be compelling models of a genuine spiritual devotion for Christian medievalists such as Lewis and Tolkien.

The Influence of High Medieval English Literature on Tolkien

Despite everything I have written thus far, Tolkien was also indebted to High Medieval English literature and its worldview. What were the origins and distinctives of that worldview? By the fourteenth century, Christian minds had meditated on the Scriptures and on the theological implications of Christianity for many hundreds of years—and also on Augustine and other church fathers, and on some crucial classical texts. By the time of Aquinas, Dante, and Chaucer, a great "medieval world-picture" had been constructed. The twelfth through the fourteenth centuries were also the time of the Gothic cathedral, the age of chivalry, and the birth of Romantic Love as a central value in Western civilization. By the time of the literature that we call High Medieval, the affirmation of "the design of Metod [God]" not only counterbalanced the darkness of temporal life, but even caught temporality itself up into the heavenly reality, with little remainder—just as the brutality and ugliness of Dante's *Inferno* ceases to impinge upon the experience of the redeemed Everyman who enjoys the beatific vision of Christ at the end of the *Paradiso*. (Evil literally is "nothing" at that point.)

Tolkien was deeply influenced by the High Medieval worldpicture and by the great works of High Medieval literary art, from which he borrowed heavily in his imagining of Middleearth and the quest of the Nine, although he did not borrow the triumphant Christian cosmology and worldview of this period. High Medieval Arthurian chivalric literature is frequently recalled in *The Silmarillion,* of course, but also in *The Lord of the Rings'* love stories (especially the courtly romance of Éowyn and Faramir, which echoes Chaucer's *Knight's Tale*) and in the descriptions of the Elvish realms and their courtly gentle-folk. Great dream-visions and encyclopedic frame-stories were also typical of the period, informed by the stirring incarnational theology of Thomas Aquinas and invigorated by the work of the great teaching orders, the Dominicans and the Franciscans, who taught the Gospel even among the poorest in society.

Tolkien, while intimately acquainted with all of the great works and movements of the High Medieval period, used his own scholarly life to work primarily on the works of a lesserknown (but equally brilliant) English contemporary of Chaucer, the nameless Northwest Midlands poet who wrote *The Pearl* and *Sir Gawain and the Green Knight*, and several other Middle English works of such exquisite beauty that there is no way I can begin to convey it to you. (Once, I ordered Tolkien's critical edition of *Pearl* and *Gawain* and made my undergraduate students read both poems in their difficult original dialect of Middle English. Some of my students have never let me forget that I did that, but at least they admit that they were thereby able to *begin* to appreciate the unmatched intricacy and beauty and finesse of which the *Pearl*-poet was capable. Tolkien was still working on his own translations of these works when he died.)

Like Anglo-Saxon literature, High Medieval literature coincided with a time of intense Christian spirituality and renewal; the *Pearl*-poet, for example, shows the influence of the Wycliffite revival going on at Oxford in the poet's lifetime, with its critique of ecclesiastical legalism and its dual emphasis on salvation by grace and on the availability of a vernacular Bible. (Like King Alfred, John Wycliffe was much concerned to give English laypersons the Scriptures in their own tongue, and hundreds of Middle English manuscript Bibles survive from this period.) The staggeringly enormous cultural synthesis reflected in the literature (Lewis says the medievals were distinguished by their love of books and their love of order: they would have liked the Dewey decimal system!) was the culmination of almost 1000 years of Western Christian thought and practice; its outlook was notably different from the Anglo-Saxon. I think of it as a period of naked human thought, thought aspiring to be thoroughly Christian and to integrate all that was known into one great system, erected upon the basis of revelation. Like the cathedrals and the universities that it founded, this culture was aspiring if not soaring: its genres were largely, ambitiously inclusive, encyclopedic: we see the lengthy narratives of the chivalric romance, the long dream-visions or frame-stories gathering together many, many stories and reflecting profoundly upon them all, as in *The Canterbury Tales* or *The Divine Comedy*. In the largest sense, High Medieval literature was imbued with the upward-soaring spirit and the plenitudinous details that also went into the Gothic style or the boldly syncretistic and highly complex Ptolemaic world-picture. As an account of the entire cosmos this latter was surely one of the very greatest of those collective works of the human imagination that emerge from time to time out of a civilization, as for example in our own period we have seen the revolutionary ways that relativity theory and quantum mechanics have mapped out the physics of the very large and the very small. (Physicist and humanist Abraham Bronowski has said that the way physicists worked together at modeling the interior of the atom during the first half of the twentieth century produced the century's greatest creative work of art.)

Celebrating Middle-earth

The High Medieval worldview was upward-tending, educative, and paradoxically both hierarchical and egalitarian—and most of all it founded itself on the cosmic dynamics of love, the desire of Creator for the Created and vice versa, the "links and contradictions of loves human and divine."[4] The sense of the higher divine order in the heavens, beyond the moon, in spite of the evident disorganization and sorrow of human experience "below the moon," is so pervasive in this period that it seems even to have been applied to the construction of the mazes which were laid out on the floors of some cathedrals, and were walked by pilgrims on their knees, as the final painful stage of their pilgrimages. That is, in recent times, it has been realized that these formless mazes, if viewed from a distance high above the cathedral roofs (whence no medieval eye could view them) actually would resolve themselves into the master-image of the supernatural order: the heavenly Rose that represents the spiritual Church Universal. That is to say, what is experienced by sublunar, mortal human beings as anguish and confusion, when seen from a God's-eye perspective, turns out to have conformed all along to the perfect contours of God's Providential design.

Tolkien both revered and, I think, suspected such a gloriously triumphant cosmic consolation. The trouble with it for him was that the reality of loss and defeat might indeed seem to fade away and "cease to be finally important." Such a condition might be appropriate for a Christian in heaven, but not for any mortal human while here on this earth. For the medievalist Tolkien, the Christian worshipper is as much one as the other here on earth. (While the natural "laws of *kynde*" are not the highest laws, they are still laws for all creatures, each according to its *kynde*, as we see in Ransom's decision to return to earth in Lewis's *Out of the Silent Planet*.) While a Christian may be a kind of amphibian, living out a natural and a spiritual life simultaneously, the higher reality of the spiritual is no excuse for "un-*kynde*-ness."

In fact, though, the fourteenth-century dream-vision Tolkien chose to edit and to translate, the Middle English *Pearl*, goes even further. Not only is this work remarkable in giving equal or even greater weight to the mortal human experience of love-longing and loss than to the higher spiritual consolation offered by a divine vision (a contrast to the more typical High Medieval movement away from nature and into grace seen in Dante), but the poem also explicitly recognizes our mortal attachments as the very means of grace used by God to educate and fulfill the human heart. To be sure, Tolkien did draw upon the cathedral-like, numinous, upward-aspiring poetry of the High Medieval period, just as he drew upon the dark elegiac of the Anglo-Saxon world. But he did not adopt the totalizing certainty of its triumphant cosmic vision.

The Lord of the Rings is in a certain sense a frame-story in the High Medieval sense: its linear narrative provides an opportunity for the artist to create an encyclopedic gathering of songs and stories which can proliferate within that narrative frame (and still leave enough of a remainder for *The Silmarillion* and other posthumous publications). This narrative ambitiousness and inclusivity was surely important to Tolkien, but while *The Lord of the Rings* is generically reminiscent of High Medieval works, nevertheless Tolkien's rich amalgam of narratives is being used for the same purposes that historical allusions are used by the *Beowulf*-poet: to create a sense of pastness and melancholy depth within which the heroic-elegiac courage can be accorded its fitting weight. While the chivalric romance is alive and well in Middle-earth, and while it seems to me that the Elvish realms partake particularly of the atmosphere of the "perilous realm" of the Fairie Otherworld encountered in High Medieval, Celtic-inspired chivalric works such as *Sir Gawain and the Green Knight* and other medieval romances of knights and their ladies, the fact remains that Tolkien chose to place all of his characters and the entire long narrative of their almost-hopeless journey, in an ancient elegiac context, rather than in the explicitly Christian worldview of the High Medieval synthesis (drawn on, for example, by Lewis for the fictional worlds of the Ransom novels and for the chronicles of Narnia).

Blended Legacies

In general, then, we can say that Tolkien used most of the genres of the Old and Middle English literatures: both their literary forms and their conventions. Secondly, and most fascinatingly to me, he chose to place his action within a world that was primarily Anglo-Saxon rather than High Medieval. Tolkien used Anglo-Saxon literature for the earthliness of Middle-earth, in the Shire and in the stout warriors of dwarvedom and of Gondor and Rohan, and he used High Medieval literature for the gleams of transcendence in Middle-earth—in the high chivalric courtly life of Rohan and Gondor and the otherworldliness of Lothlórien, Rivendell, and the men of the Númenorean line.

Yet, while it seems clear that Tolkien borrowed from High Medieval literature for his Elvish and Númenorean histories and characters, nevertheless the most important fact is that he set his tale deliberately within the darker Anglo-Saxon elegiac worldview, in which the follower of the good is forced to chose sides in the face of almost certain defeat of the good, without any definitive assurance of a future consolation or higher resolution. The absence of overt religious practice or worship of a divine Maker in *The Lord of the Rings* has been much remarked, especially in view of Tolkien's own lifelong adherence to Catholic Christianity, but I think that the best explanation for it may lie in Tolkien's deliberate choice of the darker Anglo-Saxon elegiac worldview as the setting for the adventures of Frodo and Aragorn and the Company. I think that, like C. S. Lewis (and like most Christians of the earlier, pre-modern periods), Tolkien perceived a danger in too triumphalist a version of the Christian hope. It is salutary to consider, for example, the final writings before death of martyrs such as Tyndale and Thomas More, as Lewis writes of them in a chapter of his volume of *The Oxford History of English Literature*, entitled *The Sixteenth Century, Excluding Drama.* Even martyrdom does not insure a properly Christian death, for pride might supplant humility in the heart of the martyr even in the moment of martyrdom itself. Humility and awareness of human weakness were seen by earlier Christians as the essence of genuine sanctity; this older view was very unlike the potential "hedonism" that sometimes passes for Christianity, but is a distortion of its message. Such hedonism, or indulgent self-serving, would occur if believers were to accept the Good News about Christ in order to avoid calamity and to be on the winning side, "believing" for the sake of gaining eternal rewards. To an artist and a Christian such as Tolkien, Christian devotion entails a spirituality much more like the battlefield heroism celebrated by the Anglo-Saxons, when they based their actions not on their own survival or success, but on a personal loyalty to the goodness of a master whose goodness is best seen in the moment in which master has fallen before the enemy. Loving the Good for its own sake, *even in its defeat,* offers for Tolkien the purest essence of what faith in Christ means: hence the many kinds and degrees of loyalty and hope that govern the actions of the Nine and all those in the armies of Middle-earth, who oppose the Dark Lord in spite of the absence of overt religion in Middle-earth's Third Age.

Furthermore, Tolkien does not need to sketch in religion in the Third Age of Middle-earth because Middle-earth is inherently a biblical universe. This status or identification of it does not depend in any way upon whether or not a Creator God or a sacrificial Saviour is explicitly mentioned in it. The patterns of incarnationalism and vicarious atonement are present everywhere in *The Lord of the Rings*: they are powerfully present and they are *dissolved into the story.* (Of any mythical universe, that of *Star Wars* for example, or *Harry Potter*, we may ask whether the fictional world appears to be a monistic one, or a dualistic one, or a fatalistic one. My own view is that *Star Wars* is strongly dualistic, while the *Henry Potter* world gives many hints of being monistic and incarnational.)

Tolkien's world, in its "inner consistency of reality," is one that consistently evidences an Augustinian Christian understanding of the nature of Being and the nature of Evil. Middle-earth is not the scene of a dualistic struggle between forces of Good and Evil, but a world whose plenitude of *kyndes* bespeak their common origins in a sacred source of goodness. Every evil thing in Middle-earth was originally, once upon a time, a good thing. Orcs and trolls have come into being through Sauron's cruel mutilations of Elves and Ents, through the deliberate tormenting and ruining of their original natures. (The Peter Jackson scenes of the transformation of Orthanc, beginning with the uprooting of the great trees, are especially powerful in showing these principles in action.) Saruman, originally "the White," devolves into the fallen Saruman "of Many Colors." Once the nine Ringwraiths had been good and noble kings among men; originally, the mallorn trees had flowered and the rings had been honestly crafted. In Middle-earth, Evil is not primary, but secondary, and comes along as parasitic upon the original goodness of creation, and we would know this even without the scriptural theology of *The Silmarillion's* creation myth (*Ainulindale*) to guide us explicitly to this conclusion. Evil comes into existence as the lessening of what is inherently good in its nature, or by the invasion and twisting of inherent powers, just as some of the trees turn inward and grow silent despite their shepherd Treebeard's ministrations. But in their original "kindliness," all things in Middle-earth were made to thrive, and to thrive differently from one another. Legolas is as refreshed by wandering amidst the trees as Gimli is by sleep; the wild men on the margins of lands of the Rohirrim keep their own kind of faith, while the Rohirrim live by other rules. Nothing is originally bad, only turning bad over time by a crippling of its nature.

Middle-earth is resoundingly a monistic universe: a world ontologically of a single nature or stuff which is good in a rich variety of ways of being: the kind of universe described for us in *Genesis*. As the shadow of un-nature or denatured being (compare Lewis's Unman in *Perelandra* or the Head in *That Hideous Strength*) spreads across the lands of Middle-earth, the ways of resistance are bound to be the ways of rootedness, of clinging to the best of the past and to the rich particularity of each kind of life. While a hierarchy of goodnesses may be seen, yet the presence of the higher does not demean the lower: the biblical focus on the humble, lifted by grace above the most sublime, operates abundantly in Middle-earth, as at the Council of Elrond. Finally, the greatest evils must infallibly derive from the ruination of the greatest goods: Saruman as the head of the wizardly order becomes in his ruinous fall a powerful evil indeed; the lesser wizard Gandalf, in his sacrificial fall, is lifted up into a greater sphere of power and goodness than Saruman had previously attained.

Even without Gandalf's hints about a larger purposiveness operating in the history of Middle-earth, then, Middle-earth reveals itself in its own workings as a created world whose distinctive *kyndes* reflect their making by an unseen Source of being. It is also a universe of grace, a world whose moral laws operate through choosing the humblest to bring succor to the apparently most sublime. Rootedness, simplicity, inconsequence—these are the characteristics that suit simple

Hobbits (Frodo and Sam) for their great quest. The highest and greatest of Middle-earth are too vulnerable to the warping that would use their good aspirations to destroy them; only a very small and humble goodness may perchance succeed where the greatest are bound to fail. This active biblical dynamic of inverted hierarchy lifts Gandalf above Saruman as Gandalf the White, and makes the least noble and most forgotten of all Middle-earth's higher creatures, the improbable agents of its redemption. The Fellowship of the Nine and each of its individual members are sustained only by the merest glimpse of hope, clinging to the slender possibility of a scarcely-looked-for deliverance. Each of their acts and choices is a single filament woven into a dense web, so that "many paths and errands meet" in mysterious synchronicities far beyond what any creature including Gandalf or Galadriel understands. At the same time, however, the entirety of the plan will hang at various points, all of it, upon the single choice of a single creature. This hidden Providence is related to the High Medieval confidence in the efficacious workings of divine design in every human drama of choice, yet Tolkien gives it a peculiar poignancy by keeping it veiled, by shrouding it in the dark atmosphere of elegiac anguish endemic among the Anglo-Saxons, who feel always the keenness of "that touch upon the heart which sorrows have that are both poignant and remote."

Invoking this interpretive framework for Tolkien's distinctive choices and borrowings from the Anglo-Saxon and High Medieval literary worlds, I think that I can make one final observation about one of Tolkien's literary achievements that may be all his own. I find that a singular alchemy, peculiar to Tolkien, arises through his taking the love and yearning for the sea that is so characteristic of the Old English elegies (and that was little in evidence by the time of the High Medieval period) and pouring it into the hearts of his High Elvish characters. This happens, for example, when a character such as Legolas, whom I have argued much reflects the Faeirie knights peopling the High Medieval chivalric romance, is so completely captured by the cry of the gull. After all, Lothlórien is itself recognizably High Medieval: the gem-like blue and silver forest in which the *Pearl*-maiden dwells comes at once to mind. While Hobbits and dwarves employ swords and hatchets, the weapons of the early iron age, Elves enter combat with the later medieval weaponry of bows and arrows, and they appear riding horses whose tinkling caparisons remind us of the Arthurian Faerie knights we still encounter in Spenser. But when Legolas falls prey to the call of the sea, or when Galadriel feels the anguish of the coming sundering, and when each realizes that exile from Middle-earth is now inevitable, it seems to me that Tolkien is making his own original contribution to world mythology and to the Christian mythopoeic imagination. I am not aware of another meditation similar to Tolkien's upon the nature of a people who are "doomed" to immortality. Tolkien's Elves envy the mortal kinds their mortality, because they live and die with Middle-earth and therefore are not severed from her as the Elves are fated to be. The immortality of the Elves condemns them to a unique species of loss of Middle-earth, since her ages are withering away and her days are numbered, while theirs are not. Unless they are killed in battle or surrender their immortality for the sake of a mortal beloved, the Elves go on in other realms far off to the West, beyond the fields of time.

This is a striking and beautiful paradox: that immortality might sever a creature from the planet earth, while our mortality weds us to her goodness in ways immortal creatures might desire to participate. In any case, always the Elvish peoples are severed from Middle-earth in a manner in which dwarves and men and Hobbits are not, severed by the fact that their destinies and life-lines merge only for a time with the ages of Ilúvator's beautiful but temporal universe.

This location of the most anguished elegiac experience in the hearts of the Elves, where it dwells with a different kind of poignancy than in the heart of a mortal heroic-elegiac figure such as Aragorn—this imbuing of the Elvish peoples with the fateful yearning for the sea that historically occurs among the earlier Anglo-Saxons and pulls them away from all they know, is a powerful product of Tolkien's artistic vision and the working out of the "inner consistency" of his imagined world along profoundly theological lines.

And the link that makes it work, I believe, is the link between yearning for the sea and Art itself, Art as the mediation that embodies love for the beauty of this world and desire for those far-off gleams of a higher world. It seems to me that we need to consider what Tolkien writes about the Anglo-Saxon artist, as artist, for it will help us to feel the links of any artist with the Elvish peoples of Middle-earth. In his essay on *Beowulf*, Tolkien indulges in a telling little allegory about the *Beowulf* industry, in which he pictures the entire literary establishment as an unruly group of neighbors who interfere after a man takes some stones from an ancient ruin and builds himself a tower. The man's neighbors come along and push the tower over, in their frenzy to learn about the more ancient site and to "search for hidden inscriptions." Finally, after they have thrown the tower entirely down, they exclaim over "what a muddle" the tower is in, and wonder at the stupidity of the man who built it. The final line of Tolkien's story is his punch line: "But from the top of that tower the man had been able to look out upon the sea."

If one has read "The Seafarer" and "The Wanderer," one has experienced just how mythic, or largely symbolic, taken as a whole, the Anglo-Saxon love of the sea can be. The yearnings for it, which call the elegiac speakers away from the comforts of this world, are the yearnings of all hearts for whatever is ever-lastingly commensurate with the gleams of transcendence both within and beyond earthly experience. The way may be harsh and difficult, but something outside the darkness calls to the hearts that have experienced earthly love. There is the witness of a memory. The witness of a hope. The tower enables us to see both ahead and behind.

The tower Tolkien's man built out of older materials, and which his neighbors did not bother to climb before they disassembled it for their own purposes, is of course a poem, in this case, *Beowulf*. It is also Everypoem. The tower is Art itself, and what it ever brings to the human community is a glimpse of the sea. This is why the High Elves of Rivendell and Lothlórien *must* long for the sea. Tolkien sensed it and made it that way: the Elvish peoples are symbolically the smithies of the beautiful; they are the conveyers of unearthly beauty and of unearthly tales of earthly beauty. The Elves remember and mourn the beauty of the earth as once it was, when the First-born set out and the mallorn trees flowered. It is not that the other peoples of Middle-earth do not have art: the dwarves fashion beauty underground and the men of Dunedain passes down the old stories and Bilbo writes the old tales in his book. But the Elves do not simply make art; they *are* art. They are the tower that links Middle-earth with its roots in the Edenic past and lifts it high enough to hear far-off the calling of the sea.

We who have experienced Middle-earth have been given the bittersweet irony of knowing that the very creatures who in their immortal natures are most destined for transcendence, most detached as it were from the earthly, most destined for the happy realms of Westerness over the sea, who are most caught in anguish between their love of Middle-earth and their yearning for the sea which calls them away from it. That equipoise or "cross-biasing" of the Elvish heart is similar in poignancy and interest to the *fusion* Tolkien shows us in the mind of the *Beowulf*-poet, caught in his own pregnant moment of poise between past and future. Tolkien shows us in the *Beowulf*-poet, the mind and work of an artist who is removed from the doom of the pagan past, but who yet pays tribute to its defeated valor with a full heart. If such attachment is in the Elvish heart, and if it is in the heart of the *Beowulf*-poet, then it is in the heart and mind and work of Tolkien, who also has given us a tower, from which we can see the sea.

Endnotes

1   This is a phrase used by Tolkien to describe the effect of a "true tale of Faerie" in his essay, "On Fairy-Stories" in *The Tolkien Reader* (New York: Ballantine Books, 1966).
2   "*Beowulf*: The Monsters and the Critics," reprinted in. *An Anthology of* Beowulf *Criticism*, ed. Lewis E. Nicholson (Notre Dame, Indiana: University of Notre Dame Press, 1963). All quoted material is from this essay unless otherwise noted.
3   Tolkien describes this verse form as being not based upon a "tune" but upon a "balance," built up like "masonry" out of the half-line building blocks. His description in the *Beowulf* essay would be helpful to those trying to perform the poetry of Middle-earth.
4   Norman F. Cantor, *Medieval History: The Life and Death of a Civilization*, second edition (New York: Macmillan, 1969).

4

True Myth

The Catholicism of
The Lord of the Rings

Joseph Pearce

J. R. R. Tolkien's *The Lord of the Rings* has emerged as "the greatest book of the twentieth century" in several major polls conducted in recent years. In a poll of more than 25,000 British bibliophiles, conducted jointly by a major bookselling chain and a national television channel, Tolkien's myth triumphed over all opposition. One-fifth of all people polled nominated *The Lord of the Rings* as their first-place choice. It was a runaway winner, securing 1,200 votes more than George Orwell's *Nineteen Eighty-four*, its nearest rival.[1] A similar poll, conducted by the *Daily Telegraph*, confirmed Tolkien's dominance. He was voted the twentieth century's greatest author, ahead of George Orwell and Evelyn Waugh in second and third place respectively. Two months later, a poll of the fifty thousand members of the Folio Society produced an even more staggering vindication of the literary position of *The Lord of the Rings*. The Folio Society asked its members to name their favourite books of any age, not simply those published in the twentieth century, and Tolkien's myth triumphed once again. It received 3,270 votes. Jane Austen's *Pride and Prejudice* was second with 3,212 votes and *David Copperfield* by Charles Dickens was third with 3,070 votes.[2]

Tolkien's triumph was greeted with anger and contempt by many literary "experts." The writer Howard Jacobson reacted with splenetic scorn, dismissing Tolkien as being "for children... or the adult slow." The poll merely demonstrated "the folly of teaching people to read.... It's another black day for British culture."[3] Susan Jeffreys, writing in *The Sunday Times*, described *The Lord of the Rings* as "a horrible artifact" and added that it was "depressing... that the votes for the world's best twentieth-century book should have come from those burrowing an escape into a nonexistent world."[4] Similarly, Griff Rhys Jones on the BBC's Bookworm programme appeared to believe that Tolkien's epic went no deeper than the "comforts and rituals of childhood."[5] *The Times Literary Supplement* described the results of the poll as "horrifying,"[6] while a writer in *The Guardian* complained that *The Lord of the Rings* "must be by any reckoning one of the worst books ever written."[7]

Probably the most bitter response to Tolkien's triumph came from the feminist writer, Germaine Greer, best-known for her authorship of the best-selling handbook of women's "liberation," *The Female Eunuch*. Greer complained that the enduring success of *The Lord of the Rings* was a nightmare come true.

> As a fifty-seven-year-old lifelong teacher of English, I might be expected to regard this particular list of books of the century with dismay. I do. Ever since I arrived at Cambridge as a student in 1964 and encountered a tribe of full-grown women wearing puffed sleeves, clutching teddies and babbling excitedly about the doings of hobbits, it has been my nightmare that Tolkien would turn out to be the most influential writer of the twentieth century. The bad dream has materialized. At the head of the list, in pride of place as the book of the century, stands *The Lord of the Rings*.[8]

Rarely has a book caused such controversy; rarely has the vitriol of the critics highlighted to such an extent the cultural schism between the literary illuminati and the views of the reading public.

It is perhaps noteworthy that most of the self-styled "experts" amongst the literati who have queued up to sneer contemptuously at *The Lord of the Rings* are outspoken champions of cultural deconstruction and moral relativism. Most would treat the claims of the Catholic Church with the same dismissive disdain with which they have poured scorn upon Tolkien. If, however, the secularist prejudices of Tolkien's critics should cause Christians to pause for thought, they should not blind them to the merits or otherwise of Tolkien's work. After all, our enemy's enemy is not necessarily our friend.

Some Christians remain suspicious of *The Lord of the Rings*. They see within its mythological setting, hints of neo-paganism, possibly even Satanism. Can anything containing wizards and elves, and sorcery and magic, be trusted? Certainly, in the wake of the worldwide success of the Harry Potter books, many Christians fear the effect that "fantasy" literature might be having on their children. Are these fears justified? Should Christian parents prohibit their children from reading these books? Emphatically, in the case of *The Lord of the Rings* at least, the answer to these questions is "No." Far from being prohibited, Tolkien's epic should be required reading in every Christian family. It should take its place beside the Narnian Chronicles of C. S. Lewis (Tolkien's great friend) and the fairy-stories of George MacDonald as an indispensable part of a Christian childhood.

It is intriguing that the same Christians who express their suspicion of Tolkien are quite happy for their children to be exposed to the witches and the magic in C. S. Lewis's stories. Clearly these naturally concerned parents are oblivious of the profound Christianity that threads its way through Tolkien's myth. In truth, and "truth" is the operative word, the power of Christ speaks more potently and subtly in Tolkien's Middle-earth than in Lewis's Narnia.

The profoundly Christian nature and super-nature of Tolkien's work can be demonstrated by adopting a tri-focal approach. First, by looking at Tolkien the man we shall discover the soul of a Christian mystic; second, by studying Tolkien's philosophy of myth we shall come to understand the theological basis of his own mythological world; and third, by looking at the myth itself, as revealed in *The Silmarillion* and *The Lord of the Rings*, we shall see that Tolkien's epic goes beyond mere "fantasy" to the deepest realms of metaphysics. Far from being an escapist fantasy, *The Lord of the Rings* will be revealed as a theological thriller.

Tolkien the Man

In order to get to grips with Tolkien the man—or as Tolkien as the man behind the myth of *The Lord of the Rings*—it is useful to start with how the man saw himself. Specifically, it is useful to see how he saw himself in relation to his work. In a letter written shortly after *The Lord of the Rings* was published, Tolkien wrote that "only one's guardian Angel, or indeed God Himself, could unravel the real relationship between personal facts and an author's works."[9] Nonetheless, and having dismissed the pseudo-Freudian dabblings of "so-called 'psychologists'," Tolkien confessed that there was "a scale of significance" in the biographical "facts" of an author's life. He then divided the "facts" of his own life into three distinct categories, namely the "insignificant," the "more significant" and the "really significant."

> There are insignificant facts (those particularly dear to analysts and writers about writers): such as drunkenness, wife-beating, and suchlike disorders. I do not happen to be guilty of these particular sins. But if I were, I should not suppose that artistic work proceeded from the weakness that produced them, but from other and still uncorrupted regions of my being. Modern 'researchers' inform me that Beethoven cheated his publishers, and abominably ill-treated his nephew; but I do not believe that has anything to do with his music.

Apart from these "insignificant facts," Tolkien believed that there were "more significant facts, which *have* some relation to an author's works." In this category he placed his academic vocation as a philologist at Oxford University. This had affected his "taste in languages" which was "obviously a large ingredient in *The Lord of the Rings*." Yet even this was subservient to more important factors:

> And there are a few basic facts, which however drily expressed, are really significant. For instance I was born in 1892 and lived for my early years in 'the Shire' in a pre-mechanical age. Or more important, I am a Christian (which can be deduced from my stories), and in fact a Roman Catholic.

Thus, according to Tolkien's own "scale of significance," his Catholic faith was the most important, or most "significant," influence on the writing of *The Lord of the Rings*. It is, therefore, not merely erroneous but patently perverse to see Tolkien's epic as anything other than a specifically Christian myth. This being so, and considering how the very concept of "myth" is often misunderstood, we should proceed to a discussion of Tolkien's philosophy of myth.

Tolkien's Philosophy of Myth

Tolkien's development of the philosophy of myth derives directly from his Christian faith. In fact, to employ a lisping pun, Tolkien is a *mis*understood man precisely because he is a *myth*understood man. He understood the nature and meaning of myth in a manner which has not been grasped by his critics. It is this misapprehension on the part of his critics that lies at the very root of their failure to appreciate his work. For most modern critics a myth is merely another word for a lie or a falsehood, something which is intrinsically *not* true. For Tolkien, myth had virtually the opposite meaning. It was the only way that certain transcendent truths could be expressed in intelligible form. This paradoxical philosophy was destined to have a decisive and profound influence on C. S. Lewis, facilitating his conversion to Christianity.

When Lewis and Tolkien had first met, Lewis was beginning to perceive the inadequacy of the agnosticism into which he had lapsed, having previously discarded any remnants of childhood Christianity. By the summer of 1929 he had renounced agnosticism and professed himself a theist, believing in the existence of God but denying the claims of Christianity. Essentially, this was his position when, in September 1931, he had the discussion with Tolkien, and their mutual friend, Hugo Dyson, which was destined to have a revolutionary impact on his life. After dinner the three men went for a walk and discussed the nature and purpose of myth. Lewis explained that he felt the power of myths but that they were ultimately untrue.[10] As he expressed it to Tolkien, myths were "lies and therefore worthless, even though breathed through silver."

"No," Tolkien replied. "They are not lies."

Tolkien argued that, far from being lies, myths were the best way of conveying truths which would otherwise be inexpressible. We have come from God and inevitably the myths woven by us, though they contain error, reflect a splintered fragment of the true light, the eternal truth that is with God. Myths may be misguided, but they steer however shakily towards the true harbour, whereas materialistic "progress" leads only to the abyss and to the power of evil.

Building on this philosophy of myth, Tolkien and Dyson went on to express their belief that the story of Christ was simply a true myth, a myth that works in the same way as the others, but a myth that really happened. Whereas pagan myths revealed fragments of eternal truth through the words of poets, the True Myth of Christianity revealed the whole truth through the Word Himself. The poets of pagan antiquity told their story with words, but God, the omnipotent Poet, told the True Story with facts—weaving His tale with the actions of real men in actual history.

Tolkien's arguments had an indelible effect on Lewis. The edifice of his unbelief crumbled and the foundations of his Christianity were laid. Twelve days later Lewis wrote to a friend that he had "just passed on from believing in God to definitely believing in Christ—in Christianity.... My long night talk with Dyson and Tolkien had a good deal to do with it."[11] It is interesting—indeed astonishing—to note that without J. R. R. Tolkien there might not have been C. S. Lewis, at least not the C. S. Lewis that has come to be known and loved throughout the world as the formidable Christian apologist and author of sublime Christian myths, such as *The Lion, the Witch and the Wardrobe*.

Integral to Tolkien's philosophy of myth was the belief that creativity was a mark of God's divine image in Man. God, as Creator, poured forth the gift of creativity to men, the creatures created in His own image. Only God could Create in the primary sense, i.e. by bringing something into being out of nothing. Man, however, could sub-create by moulding the material of Creation into works of beauty. Music, art and literature were all acts of sub-creation expressive of the divine essence in man. In this way, men shared in the Creative power of God. This sublime vision found (sub)creative expression in the opening pages of *The Silmarillion*, the enigmatic and unfinished work that forms the theological and philosophical foundation upon which, and the mythological framework within which, *The Lord of the Rings* is structured.

The Silmarillion delved deep into the past of Middle-earth, Tolkien's sub-created world, and the landscape of legends recounted in its pages formed the vast womb of myth from which *The Lord of the Rings* was born. Indeed, Tolkien's *magnum opus* would not have been born at all if he had not first created, in *The Silmarillion*, the world, the womb, in which it was conceived.

The most important part of *The Silmarillion* is its account of the Creation of Middle-earth by the One. This Creation myth is perhaps the most significant, and the most beautiful, of all Tolkien's work. It goes to the very roots of his creative vision and says much about Tolkien himself. Somewhere within the early pages of *The Silmarillion* is to be found both the man behind the myth and the myth behind the man.

Tolkien's Myth Revealed

The "myth" behind Tolkien was, of course, Catholic Christianity, the "True Myth," and it is scarcely surprising that Tolkien's own version of the Creation in *The Silmarillion* bears a remarkable similarity to the Creation story in the book of Genesis. In the beginning was Eru, the One, who "made first the Ainur, the Holy Ones, that were the offspring of his thought, and they were with him before aught else was made."[12] God, the One, "spoke to them, propounding to them themes of music." He then allows the Holy Ones, or Archangels, to share his Creative gifts, declaring to them their role in Creation: "Of the theme that I have declared to you, I will now that ye make in harmony together a Great Music. And since I have kindled you with the Flame Imperishable, ye shall show forth your powers in adorning this theme, each with his own thoughts and devices, if he will." In this way, the Archangels brought forth the Creation of God as a Symphony of Praise in His honour: "and a sound arose of endless interchanging melodies woven in harmony that passed beyond hearing into the depth and into the heights… and the music and the echo of the music went out into the Void, and it was not void."[13]

Disharmony is brought into the cosmic symphony of Creation when one of the Archangels decides to play his own tune in defiance of the will of the Composer. Instead of being an instrument in the Great Music, the Rebel Archangel composes his own theme, bringing discord. This disharmony is the beginning of evil. Again, Tolkien's myth follows the "True Myth" of Christianity with allegorical precision. The Rebel Archangel is named Melkor, later known as Morgoth, and is obviously Middle-earth's equivalent of Lucifer, also known as Satan. Melkor is described by Tolkien as "the greatest of the Ainur" as Lucifer was the greatest of the archangels. Like Lucifer, Melkor is the ultimate source of the sin of pride, intent on corrupting mankind for his own spiteful purposes. Melkor desired "to subdue to his will both Elves and Men," envious of the gifts which God had promised them, "and he wished himself to have subjects and servants, and to be called Lord, and to be master over other wills."[14]

The allegory becomes even less mistakable when Tolkien describes the war between Melkor and Manwë, who is clearly cast in the role of the archangel Michael. "And there was strife between Melkor and the other Valar; and for that time Melkor withdrew and departed to other regions and did there what he would."[15]

The parallels between Melkor and Lucifer are made even more apparent when Tolkien explains that the name, Melkor, means "He who arises in Might"—"But that name he has forfeited; and the Noldor, who among the Elves suffered most from his malice, will not utter it, and they name him Morgoth, the Dark Enemy of the World."[16] Similarly, Lucifer, brightest of all the angels, means "Light Bringer," whereas Satan, like Morgoth, means "Enemy." Tolkien's intention, both as a Christian and as a philologist, in identifying Melkor with Lucifer is plain enough.

Taking his inspiration, no doubt, from the Book of Isaiah ("Thy pomp is brought down to the grave, and the noise of thy viols: the worm is spread under thee, and the worms cover thee.

How art thou fallen from heaven, O Lucifer, son of the morning." Isaiah 14:11–12), Tolkien says of Melkor:

> From Splendour he fell through arrogance to contempt for all things save himself, a spirit wasteful and pitiless. Understanding he turned to subtlety in perverting to his own will all that he would use, until he became a liar without shame. He began with the desire of Light, but when he could not possess it for himself alone, he descended through fire and wrath into a great burning, down into Darkness. And darkness he used most in his evil works upon Arda, and filled it with fear for all living things.[17]

Apart from the scriptural influence, the other over-riding influence is Augustinian theology. Evil, as symbolized by darkness, has no value of its own but is only a negation of that which is good, as symbolized by light.

Shortly after this description of Melkor, Tolkien introduces Sauron, the Dark Enemy in *The Lord of the Rings*. Sauron is described as a "spirit" and as the "greatest" of Melkor's, alias Morgoth's, servants: "But in after years he rose like a shadow of Morgoth and a ghost of his malice, and walked behind him on the same ruinous path down into the Void."[18]

Thus, the evil powers in *The Lord of the Rings* are specified as direct descendents of Tolkien's Satan, rendering impossible, or at any rate implausible, anything but a Christian interpretation of the book. Catholic theology, explicitly present in *The Silmarillion* and implicitly present in *The Lord of the Rings*, is omnipresent in both, breathing life into the tales as invisibly but as surely as oxygen.

The sheer magnificence of Tolkien's mythological vision precludes any adequate appraisal, in an essay of this length, of the Christian mysticism and theology that gives it life. In the impenetrable blackness of the Dark Lord and his abysmal servants, the Ringwraiths, we feel the objective reality of Evil. Sauron and his servants confront and affront us with the nauseous presence of the Real Absence of goodness. In his depiction of the potency of evil, Tolkien presents the reader with a metaphysical black-hole far more unsettling than Milton's proud vision of Satan as "darkness visible."

Tolkien is, however, equally powerful in his depiction of goodness. In the unassuming humility of the Hobbits we see the exaltation of the humble. In their reluctant heroism we see a courage ennobled by modesty. In the immortality of the elves, and the sadness and melancholic wisdom it evokes in them, we receive an inkling that man's mortality is a gift of God, a gift that ends his exile in mortal life's "vale of tears" and enables him, in death, to achieve a mystical union with the Divine beyond the reach of Time.

In Gandalf we see the archetypal prefiguration of a powerful Prophet or Patriarch, a seer who beholds a vision of the Kingdom beyond the understanding of men. At times he is almost Christ-like. He lays down his life for his friends and his mysterious "resurrection" results in his transfiguration. Before his self-sacrificial "death" he is Gandalf the Grey; after his "resurrection" he reappears as Gandalf the White, armed with greater powers and deeper wisdom.

In the true, though exiled, Kingship of Aragorn we see glimmers of the hope for a restoration of truly ordained, i.e. Catholic, authority. The person of Aragorn represents the embodiment of the Arthurian and Jacobite yearning—the visionary desire for the "Return of the King" after eons of exile. The "sword that is broken", the symbol of Aragorn's kingship, is reforged at the anointed time—a potent reminder of Excalibur's union with the Christendom it is ordained to serve.

Significantly, the role of Men in *The Lord of the Rings* reflects their divine, though Fallen, nature. They are to be found amongst the Enemy's servants, though usually beguiled by deception into the ways of evil and always capable of repentance and, in consequence, redemption. Boromir, who represents Man in the Fellowship of the Ring, succumbs to the temptation to use the Ring, i.e. the forces of evil, in the naïve belief that it could be wielded as a powerful weapon against Sauron. He finally recognizes the error of seeking to use evil against evil. He dies heroically, laying down his life for his friends in a spirit of repentance.

Ultimately, *The Lord of the Rings* is a sublimely mystical Passion Play. The carrying of the Ring—the emblem of Sin—is the Carrying of the Cross. The mythological Quest is a veritable Via

Dolorosa. It is true that Tolkien's detractors, and many of his admirers, have failed to grasp this ultimate truth at the heart of his myth. Unfortunately, those that are blind to theology will continue to be blind to that which is most beautiful in *The Lord of the Rings*. One is reminded of Chesterton's complaint that, however much he sought to make the point of a story stick out like a spike, there were always some who would insist on impaling themselves on something else. Yet one is also reminded of the words of C. S. Lewis that a diligent atheist, or, for that matter, a delicate neo-pagan or agnostic, can not be too careful of what he reads. In straying too deeply into Tolkien's world he will be straying into the world of truths that he had not previously perceived. If he continues to follow the Fellowship of the Ring into the depths of Mordor and Beyond he might even come to see that the exciting truths point to the most exciting Truth of all. At its deepest he might finally understand that the Quest is, in fact, a Pilgrimage.

Endnotes

1 *The Guardian*, January 20, 1997.
2 *The Daily Telegraph*, April 23, 1997.
3 *The Sunday Times*, January 12, 1997.
4 *The Sunday Times*, January 26, 1997.
5 *Bookworm*, BBC-1, July 27, 1997.
6 *The Times Literary Supplement*, January 24, 1997.
7 *The Guardian*, January 4, 1997.
8 *W Magazine*, Winter/Spring 1997.
9 J. R. R. Tolkien, *The Letters of J. R. R. Tolkien*, ed. Humphrey Carpenter, (Boston: Houghton Mifflin, 1981), p. 288.
10 Humphrey Carpenter, *Tolkien: A Biography* (Boston: Houghton Mifflin, 1977), p. 147.
11 Humphrey Carpenter, *The Inklings* (London: George Allen and Unwin, 1978).
12 J. R. R. Tolkien, *The Silmarillion*, ed. Christopher Tolkien, (New York: Ballantine Books, 1977), p. 15.
13 Ibid., pp. 3–4.
14 Ibid., p. 8.
15 Ibid., p. 11.
16 Ibid., p. 25.
17 Ibid.
18 Ibid., p. 26.

Those who would like to explore this topic in greater depth may want to read
Joseph Pearce's *Tolkien: Man and Myth* published by Ignatius Press.

5

Theology and Morality in *The Lord of the Rings*

Kerry L. Dearborn

Many of my students are greatly surprised at the thought of pairing theology with J. R. R. Tolkien's name. When I teach classes on the Inklings, Dorothy Sayers and George MacDonald, students have little trouble discerning C. S. Lewis's, Dorothy Sayers' or George MacDonald's theology. They are often astounded, however, to hear that Tolkien took his Christian faith seriously. I read to them excerpts from Tolkien's letter to Mrs. Webster, a woman whom Tolkien seemed to fear was trying to pry personal tidbits from underneath the shield of his British reserve. Tolkien's response holds a key to both his faith and his way of communicating that faith. "I like seeing people. But I do not like giving 'facts' about myself other than 'dry' ones (which anyway are quite as relevant to my books as any other more juicy details)."[1] Besides insignificant facts (such as drunkenness or wife–beating of which he is not guilty), and significant facts (that he dislikes French and prefers Spanish to Italian), he included a category of basic facts. It is in this category that he referred to his faith. Tolkien wrote: "more important, I am a Christian (which can be deduced from my stories), and in fact a Roman Catholic. The latter 'fact' perhaps cannot be deduced."[2]

Tolkien's faith was deeply important to him, and it is something woven into the fabric of his stories, but something which must be *deduced*, or worked out. His theology is less overt than MacDonald's and Lewis's in their imaginative work, which I would argue is an aspect of Tolkien's theology, itself. MacDonald had the same arguments about the need to be more overtly theological with his Catholic friend, Lewis Carroll. In a letter that Tolkien wrote he states: "*The Lord the Rings* is of course, a fundamentally religious and Catholic work, unconsciously so at first but consciously in the revision. That is why I have not put in anything like 'religion' to cults or practices in the imaginary world, for the religion is absorbed into the story and the symbolism."[3]

I would like to address Tolkien's approach briefly through three themes. First is his desire to reflect the sacramental nature of reality, second, to smuggle truth into a realm that is hostile to that truth, and third, his desire to be a sub–creator. Morality in each area is dependent on the way in which one pursues each of these goals and desires. Although Tolkien reflects vivid belief in and experience of the world's depravity, his faith correlates more closely to Christian traditions that would affirm a vestige of the divine in creation and the *imago dei* (the image of God) in humanity rather than total depravity. Gandalf explains to Frodo in *The Fellowship of the Rings*, "Even Gollum was not wholly ruined…. There was a little corner of his mind that was still his own, and light came through it, as through a chink in the dark."[4]

1. Sacramental Theology

First, Tolkien depicted his belief in the *sacramental* nature of reality. For Tolkien as for Abraham Heschel, "there is a holiness that hovers over all things."[5] In *The Hobbit* Gandalf says of Bilbo that there is more to him than meets the eye. Even so for Tolkien, there was more to everything in creation than meets the eye. Almost everything can be a pointer to God's realm. Peter Kreeft called it anonymous grace.[6] In "On Fairy-Stories," Tolkien argued that people become dulled to this higher realm through rationalism and materialism. Life is meant to be lived as an adventure in which one is beckoned out of the narrow confines of one's presumed material security and protected rational domain to encounter the wonders that God has embedded in creation. As with Bilbo and Frodo, life has much to offer one who is willing to respond to the call of far off places and the awakening of deeper desires.[7] Thus Tolkien's *The Lord of the Ring* epic works like other good fairy-stories to call us out of our narrow protectionism and into the world of wonder. Tolkien wrote of fairy-stories that if they "awaken desire, satisfying it while often whetting it unbearably, they [have] succeeded."[8] Tolkien's work certainly does succeed.

But Tolkien was keenly aware that we are resistant to such adventures and stories. It takes Gandalf's rather persuasive skills and persistent work to dislodge Bilbo from his Hobbit hole to launch the entire epic adventure. Bilbo says to himself after hearing about the call to adventure, "Don't be a fool, Bilbo Baggins!... thinking of dragons and all that outlandish nonsense at your age!"[9] Gandalf comes for him and gives him only 10 minutes to get ready. Bilbo must leave without even the little things that make him feel normal—"without a hat, a walking stick or any money"—even to his horror "without a pocket handkerchief!"[10] Dwalin warns him, "You will have to manage without pocket handkerchiefs, and a good many other things, before you get to the journey's end." But there is grace. Dwalin softens, "As for a hat, I have got a spare hood and cloak in my luggage," and Gandalf brings "a lot of pocket-handkerchiefs, and Bilbo's pipe and tobacco."[11]

Even as Bilbo and Frodo are exposed to the wonder of the world in which they live, where trees have personalities of their own, where people and creatures express beauty and giftedness formerly unimaginable to them, they also encounter forces that would reduce everything to utilitarian function as a means of gaining power—forces that treat everything pragmatically, and so without a sacramental dignity. The reductionism of such forces has the effect of destroying the other and dehumanizing (or dehobbitizing) the self. G. K. Chesterton wrote, "The artist feels nothing is perfect unless it is personal."[12] Gollum sees everything in terms of its usefulness to him. He delights in the power the Ring gives him over others, and in the way it helps him satisfy his creaturely needs. Like any addiction, it slowly erodes Gollum's ability to see anything sacramentally, such that it might liberate him to higher service and to an ability to honor all of life. Rather everything is seen in a utilitarian way, as a means to serving his ends, until he almost destroys the very essence of the sacramental in himself. Bilbo, however, refuses to treat Gollum as one who is without value or as one deserving death or destruction. This serves both the good of Bilbo and the good of the entire Middle-earth, for Gollum's greed for the Ring eventually brings its destruction along with his own.

It is possible for the sacramental to be destroyed in oneself and in the world. There is nothing sacramental left in Mordor, there is only destructiveness and desolation. Tolkien is not sentimental in his portrayal of life. He had seen the face of Mordor from the trenches of the Battle of the Somme in World War I.[13]

2. Smuggling Approach

It was into the domain where the sacramental is either not recognized or has been destroyed that Tolkien worked to smuggle his revitalizing vision of life, even into the heart of the dark side itself.

> I would claim... to have as one object the elucidation of truth, and the encouragement of good morals in the real world by the ancient device of exemplifying them in unfamiliar embodiments, that may tend to "bring them home.[14]

Even as Bilbo is able to smuggle himself into the Smaug's lair, even as Frodo is able to penetrate into Mordor with the Ring, even so Tolkien longed to smuggle a vision of goodness and truth into the readers' lives. Tolkien was not pleased with the mechanistic and utilitarian age in which he lived. He longed for the Shire and thought of himself as a Hobbit in all but size. He too had to go on an adventure in leaving the protectiveness of his own British professorial life to become such a well-known writer. C. S. Lewis was like Gandalf for Tolkien, beckoning him ever on in his adventure of writing of *The Lord of the Rings*, such that Tolkien considered Lewis the midwife of his books. His smuggling was so effective that it pulled him repeatedly out of his own Shire, even as it drew others out in droves whose desire for this sacramental approach to life caught hold of them.

But Tolkien portrayed many perils involved in being such a smuggler. Frodo and Sam are accosted by many hideous creatures and forces. There are powers at work that would keep us operating as mechanistically and mindlessly as possible. Old Testament scholar, Walter Brueggemann writes in *The Prophetic Imagination:* "Passion as the capacity and readiness to care, to suffer, to die, and to feel is the enemy of imperial reality. Imperial economics is designed to keep people satiated so that they do not notice."[15] Dorothy Sayers concurs and in *The Man Born to be King* has Caiaphas argue: "It is the duty of statesmen to destroy the madness which we call imagination. It is dangerous. It breeds dissension, Peace, order, security—that is Rome's offer—at Rome's price."[16] Rather, Brueggemann proclaims: "The task of prophetic ministry is to nurture, nourish, and evoke a consciousness and perception alternative to the consciousness and perception of the dominant culture around us."[17] Tolkien's was a prophetic ministry, for he awakens the reader to elf-lands, and woodlands, trees and beings that remind us that we are not in control, and that there is more to life than what we sleepily regard.

3. Sub-creator Calling

Third, Tolkien was able to speak prophetically because he took seriously his own call as a sub-creator. Lewis said, in reference to *The Lord of the Rings*, "Perhaps no book yet written in the world is quite such a radical instance of what its author has elsewhere called 'sub-creation!'... Here are beauties which pierce like swords or burn like cold iron; here is a book that will break your heart."[18] Tolkien had a very high view of human creativity and of inspiration. George MacDonald didn't want to extend beyond calling people *makers.* God alone is the creator. Tolkien in "On Fairy-Stories," describes the writer of a fairy-story as a sub-creator, one who has the power to create new forms, that the old forms might be seen in new light. Tolkien created Middle-earth to show us the sacramental beauty and wonder of our own world and the ways in which sacramental grace can be crushed. He created oppressive regimes of Sauron and Saruman to clarify why truth must be smuggled in at times, to catch the enemy off-guard and to awaken those whose creativity and courage needed liberating.

It is not, however, as if Tolkien was claiming to create *ex nihilo*. His own sense of sub-creation was closely aligned with inspiration and redemption. In *On Fairy-Stories*, he asserted that a person might be directly inspired by God and given "A sudden glimpse of the underlying reality or truth."[19] He wrote of the tales in *The Silmarillion* that: "They arose in my mind as 'given' things and as they came, separately, so too the links grew…. I always had the sense of recording what was already 'there' somewhere, not of inventing."[20] Tolkien attributes much his creativity to a seed growing out of the "leaf mould of the mind: out of all that has been seen or thought or read, that has long ago been forgotten, descending into the deeps."[21] But the ability to convey "eucatastrophe"—"the far off gleam or echo of evangelium in the real world," Tolkien suggested derives from God having "redeemed the corrupt making-creatures… in a way fitting to this aspect."[22]

Because Tolkien longed to be a servant of God in his creativity, to reflect an "inner consistency of reality,"[23] his own worlds mirror God's creation, with the wonder of its beauty and diversity. Those called into the Fellowship of the Ring couldn't be more diverse. It is those who are of the dark side, the Ringwraiths, that all wear the same black capes and have lost their individuality. Those who understand the wonder of life and are courageous enough to live for that wonder can celebrate rather than be threatened by the differences. Tolkien's world mirrors God's creation in his moral imperatives as well. "Good and ill have not changed since yesteryear; nor are they one thing among Elves and Dwarves and another among Men. It is a man's part to discern them, as much in the Golden Wood as in his own house"[24] What we create as sub-creators may be used for good or for ill, and can be done for purposes of service or of domination. The Ring, when used to gain power over others, evaporates the sacramental center of one's being. But when used in service of others, the Ring is able to draw out of Bilbo and Frodo character and courage they never knew existed in them. Humans, like the Ainur in *The Silmarillion*, are given wondrous grace and responsibility to participate with God (Ilúvatar) in creating that which derives from "the imperishable flame" of the eternal God and is thus harmonious with God's own music of creation. Tolkien's view of human creativity was so high, that he wondered if it contributed to God's own creative work:

So great is the bounty with which he has been treated that he may now, perhaps, fairly dare to guess that in Fantasy he may actually assist in the effoliation and multiple enrichment of creation. All tales may come true; and yet, at the last, redeemed, they may be as like and as unlike the forms that we give them as Man, finally redeemed, will be like and unlike the fallen that we know."[25]

Many have experienced the enrichment of Tolkien's creativity smuggling truth and wonder into their lives. His imagination was fueled by his sense of the meaning and purpose of life, which he said was "to increase according to our capacity our knowledge of God by all means we have and to be moved by it to offer praise and thanks."[26] His theology may be latent and have to be deduced, but because it is narrative truth, communicated personally and relationally, it demonstrates Tolkien's compelling point to Lewis about myths. *The Lord of the Rings*, like all myths, points back to the central story in which Truth is a person and in which the Triune God demonstrates that love and relationship form the heart of all creation. Knowing God as he did, he remained humble about his immense achievement. Tolkien confessed in a letter: "A few years ago I was visited in Oxford by a man… who said, 'Of course you don't suppose, do you, that you wrote that book yourself?' Pure Gandalf! I was too well acquainted with G. to ask what he meant. I think I said, 'No, I don't suppose so any longer.' I have never since been able to suppose so. An alarming conclusion for an old philologist to draw concerning his private amusement. But not one that should puff up any one who considers the imperfections of 'chosen instruments,' and indeed what sometimes seems their lamentable unfitness for the purpose."[27] I think Tolkien in all of his success would agree with Gandalf's comments to Bilbo, when Bilbo realizes the significance of his role in fulfilling the prophecies. "You are a very fine person, Mr. Baggins, and I am very fond of you; but you are only quite a little fellow in a wide world after all."[28] "Thank goodness," responds Bilbo, and I think so would Tolkien.

Endnotes

1 Deborah W. Rogers and A. Ivor, *J. R. R. Tolkien*, (Boston: Twayne Publishers, 1980), p. 125.

2 Ibid., p. 126.

3 J. R. R. Tolkien, *The Letters of J. R. R. Tolkien*, ed. Humphrey Carpenter, (Boston: Houghton Mifflin, 1981), p. 172.

4 J. R. R. Tolkien, *The Fellowship of the Ring*, (Boston: Houghton Mifflin, 1987), p. 53.

5 Abraham Heschel, *Man is Not Alone*, (New York, Farrar, Straus & Young, 1951), p. 64.

6 Peter Kreeft, "Wartime Wisdom," remark at Celebrating Middle Earth Conference, Seattle Pacific University, November 9, 2001.

7 For example: "Then something Tookish woke up inside him, and he wished to go and see the great mountains, and heart the pine-trees and the waterfalls, and explore the caves, and wear a sword instead of a walking-stick." J. R. R. Tolkien, *The Hobbit* (London: HarperCollins, 1991), p. 22.

8 J. R. R. Tolkien, "On Fairy-Stories," *Tree and Leaf*, (Grafton, London: 1992), p. 39.

9 J. R. R. Tolkien, *The Hobbit*, (London: HarperCollins, 1991), p. 32.

10 Ibid., p. 33.

11 Ibid., p. 34.

12 G. K. Chesterton, *The Everlasting Man*, (New York: Doubleday, Image Books, 1955), p. 102.

13 For a helpful discussion of the influence of fighting in World War I on Tolkien, see Tom Shippey, Conversation on J. R. R. Tolkien, Mars Hill Audio Tape, Volume 52 September/October 2001.

14 J. R. R. Tolkien, The *Letters of J. R. R. Tolkien*, p. 194.

15 Walter, Brueggemann, *The Prophetic Imagination*, (Fortress Press, 1978), p. 41.

16 Dorothy Sayers, *The Man Born to be King*, (San Francisco: Ignatius Press, 1943), p. 297.

17 Walter, Brueggemann, *The Prophetic Imagination*, (Fortress Press, 1978), p. 13.

18 C. S. Lewis, *Time and Tide*, (August, 1954), p. 1082.

19 J. R. R. Tolkien, "On Fairy-Stories," p. 64.

20 Humphrey Carpenter, *Tolkien: A Biography* (Boston: Houghton Mifflin, 1977), p. 92.

21 Ibid., p. 126.

22 Tolkien, "On Fairy-Stories," pp. 64–65.

23 Ibid., p. 64.

24 J. R. R. Tolkien, *The Lord of the Rings*, (Boston: Houghton Mifflin, 1994), p. 428.

25 Tolkien, "On Fairy-Stories," p. 66.

26 J. R. R. Tolkien, *The Letters of J. R. R. Tolkien*, pp. 399–400.

27 Ibid., p. 413.

28 J. R. R. Tolkien, *The Hobbit*, p. 255.

6

The Lord of the Rings
and the
Meaning of Life

Phillip Goggans

Woody Allen's play "God" begins with a writer trying to think of an ending for his play. He can't come up with anything. Then a character appears with a "God-machine." It's an elaborate stage device that allows God to enter suddenly and dramatically into the action and save the hero. The writer is reluctant at first, but when he sees the demonstration with all the spectacular effects, he gets caught up in the enthusiasm and agrees to rent to the God machine for $26.50 an hour. The play within the play proceeds. It reaches its climax when an angry king is about to kill the hero of the story, a slave. He calls out for God to rescue him. Nothing happens. He calls again. Eventually, the God character is lowered, obviously strangled by the wires in the device. The panicked writer urges the actors to ad-lib the ending.

This is Allen's symbol for the universal human condition. The point of our lives is not written down; we all have to ad-lib. No one decides our place in life; that's up to us. Typically, we are afraid of this responsibility. We try to hide from it by renting a God-machine. Religion conveniently provides us with an illusion of meaning.

Contrast this with Tolkien's view. In the poignant scene when Sam grieves over his apparently dead master and agonizes over whether to take the Ring himself, a voice inside him says,

> You haven't put yourself forward; you've been put forward. And as for not being the right and proper person, why, Mr. Frodo wasn't, as you might say, nor Mr. Bilbo. They didn't choose themselves.[1]

This passage says something to every human being. We don't put ourselves forward; we are put forward. We don't choose ourselves for the role we have in life; we are chosen. We do not forge our destiny; we submit to it. It's hard to imagine a more emphatic denial of existentialism.

The Lord of the Rings is a novel about purpose. The purpose of things in the Middle-earth proceeded from the existence of an objective Good for Middle-earth. Frodo's mission was to carry the Ring to its destruction. The Fellowship of the Ring had a mission to assist Frodo. Sam had a mission as Frodo's servant. Pippin, in gratitude for Boromir's mortal sacrifice in defense of his life, dedicates his life to the service of Boromir's father Denethor. Merry, filled with love for old King Théoden, enters into his service. The Dúnedain made possible the peaceful Hobbit culture which, as Prof. Kreeft points out, was the instrument through which Sauron was defeated. Aragorn was heir to the throne of Gondor; his purpose was to reign there. Lord Denethor was the last of the line of stewards whose purpose was to reign in the absence of the rightful heir. Bilbo's discovery of the Ring had a purpose. The Orcs' capture of Merry and Pippin had a purpose. Sam's Elven rope had a purpose. The phial of Galadriel had a purpose. Even Gollum had a purpose, in the end.

Middle-earth is a world of order. Things in Middle-earth have a proper function.

Existentialists such as Allen point to *The Lord of the Rings* as an example of escapism. But they are perhaps guilty of escapism themselves. They get to think of themselves as the enlightened few who are brave enough to face the fundamental choices.

The main appeal of existentialism lies in the freedom it says we have. People like to think they are wholly free to choose how to live. Ours is a culture intoxicated with freedom. Being free to do whatever one wants—that is the great ideal. Plato says that this tends to happen in democratic countries. People come to expect political leaders to give them more and more freedom. They want their educators to tell them how free they are. Finally, he says, "their minds become so sensitive that the least vestige of restraint is resented as intolerable, till finally... in their determination to have no master, they disregard all laws, written or unwritten."[2] They're obsessed with freedom.

Existentialism is one of many current theories custom-designed for freedom addicts. Another is moral relativism, which says that people get to choose their own morality. Moral anti-realism says that there are no moral truths. Various forms metaphysical anti-realism deny objective truth altogether. Truth, such as there is, is dependent in some way on human conventions. At least metaphysical naturalism affirms truth; however, on this theory there's no transcendent authority to which one must submit. Like the other fashionable theories, it appeals directly to the contemporary obsession with freedom.

Plato says in the *Republic* that the excessive desire for freedom leads to slavery. In his chapter on the natural degeneration of democracy into tyranny, the freedom-obsessed people give absolute power to a champion whom they entrust with the task of liberating them from the oppression of the wealthy few. This champion proves to a tyrant such as they had never known. The people

> have jumped out of the frying-pan of subjection to free men into the fire of subjection to slaves, and exchanged their excessive and untimely freedom for the harshest and bitterest of servitudes, where the slave is master.[3]

The lust for freedom brings only slavery. It's an old and profound thought. Lewis treats of it The Abolition of Man. It's a main point of *The Lord of the Rings*.

We are free, to a point. We are free to accept our calling or reject it. The most inspiring thing about *The Lord of the Rings*, for me, is its heroes' monumental struggle to fulfill the mission that fate had ordained for them. They faced horrible privation, numbing fatigue, fierce monsters, mortal peril, uncertainty and despair. Nothing could make them abandon their mission. Sam's office was to serve Frodo, and he does so with supernatural ardor. The scene where he beats off Gollum and then takes on Shelob is etched in my mind forever.

Whereas the good characters all submit to authority outside of them, the bad ones recognize no authority higher than their individual will. Orcs submit to nothing unless they are forced to. Each tries to rule over the others. As a result, they constantly quarrel. Saruman and Sauron try to rule the world; each of them is a case study in the Nietzschean ethic. Lord Denethor's corruption results in his unwillingness to submit to the terms of his office as steward. Shelob and Gollum each live a hellish, isolated existence. Indeed, all the evil characters are isolated. Orcs may have massed together, but they did not live in community. Those in community must submit to the order that makes community possible.

The fundamental conflict in *The Lord of the Rings* corresponds to the great perennial conflict within the human race. One side in the conflict claims that each individual and indeed the human race itself is under a higher authority. This side seeks to conform to the order that was ordained by that authority. The other side denies any higher authority than the individual will. Speaking as one whose allegiance is to the first side, I call the other side "impious."

It's also a conflict within every human heart. We're torn between the desire to submit to a higher authority and the desire to be our own boss.

Ultimately we are subordinate to God alone. But God has placed us within a natural order. Submission to God requires respect for this order. This world, like Middle-earth, is suffused with purpose. As Aristotle said, nature makes nothing in vain. There's a reason for everything in life: joy, sadness, pride, shame and the other emotions. Pain and pleasure have a purpose. Sexuality, eating and sleep and all other biological functions have a purpose. The great events in human life have a purpose: marriage, childbirth, suffering and death. So do human activities like artistic production, play and worship. We live after the manner of Frodo and Gandalf and the other heroes of *The Lord of the Rings* if we respect the proper functions of things in the world. We subvert the natural order if we use things in ways incompatible with their natural end. The Stoic dictum "Live according to nature" urges us to cooperate with the natural order. To act in a way that frustrates that order is "contrary to natural law."

Middle-earth, with all its wizardry and monsters, is a truer picture of the real world than the worlds fantasized by existentialists and metaphysical naturalists. *The Lord of the Rings* is not escapism. Far from it. It is a strong does of reality. For there is indeed a natural order. The best we can do is to study it and try to cooperate with it.

Endnotes

1 J. R. R. Tolkien, *The Two Towers* (New York: Ballantine Books, 1965), p. 433.
2 *Republic*, VIII; 563d, trans. by Desmond Lee.
3 *Republic*, 569b, trans. by Desmond Lee.

Printed in the United States
1532000003B/175-204